MW00334417

# French & Indian
# WARS
## IN
# MAINE

# French & Indian WARS

—— *IN* ——

# MAINE

MICHAEL DEKKER

THE
History
PRESS

Published by The History Press
Charleston, SC 29403
www.historypress.net

*Front cover, top, left to right*: Wikimedia Commons, Maine Historical Society, Bowdoin College
Museum of Art; *bottom*: Maine Historical Society.
*Back cover, top and bottom*: Wikimedia Commons.

First published 2015

ISBN 978.1.5402.0223.9

Library of Congress Control Number: 2015937275

*Notice*: The information in this book is true and complete to the best of our knowledge. It is
offered without guarantee on the part of the author or The History Press. The author and
The History Press disclaim all liability in connection with the use of this book.

*For my infinitely patient and understanding family. Kathy, maybe now our schedules and routines will return to normal. Thanks for all you have done to support me in this endeavor. Whit, we have some play time to catch up on. Ellie, thanks for our evening television sessions. They were just what I needed.*

# Contents

# Preface

James Skoglund, my middle school social studies teacher, planted the seed of this book many years ago. Growing up in Thomaston and developing an early interest in history, I was naturally receptive to Mr. Skoglund's intimation that Thomaston had been a battleground among the English, the French and the Indians. Having found an old bayonet in the barn and an arrowhead in the garden as a young boy, my imagination was primed and my interest piqued. Twenty-five years later, I took up reenacting as a hobby, portraying a soldier on the Maine frontier during the French and Indian War. At the time, I knew Massachusetts had built forts along the Kennebec River and provided soldiers to garrison the outposts scattered across the region. While attending a battle reenactment at Fort Ticonderoga, an unknown fellow reenactor asked me "Why do you portray a soldier in Maine? Nothing happened there." I distinctly remember replying, "That may be true, but the men manning cold, isolated outposts deserve to be remembered in the same way as those who participated in the grand, memorable events of the war." Feeling comfortable with the answer, the question itself left me feeling unsettled. The memory of Mr. Skoglund's words years before gave me pause to consider that perhaps more happened in Maine during the period than I or most people realized.

Combing the records of local historical societies, town histories, the collections of the Maine Historical Society and the Massachusetts Archives, I sought a more complete understanding of the French and

Indian War here in Maine. Initially, I began cataloguing incidents and events pertaining to King George's War (1745–48) and the French and Indian War (1755–63). The cursory and incomplete list quickly topped 125 examples of armed encounters between white and native people who called Maine home. It became readily apparent that both the question asked of me at Ticonderoga and my answer were ill founded. Maine was not a quiet backwater on the periphery of the struggle for North America. Rather, Maine, and the midcoast region in particular, was caught up in its own related but distinctly local struggle between competing cultures.

All history occurs within a context. As it was, I began my inquiry at the end of a historic epoch. King George's War and the French and Indian War were the final chapters in a long, sad story of war, dependence, disease and displacement. The tragedy began with the very first exchanges between Europeans and the native people of eastern North America and would continue in Maine for the next 150 years. Staggering from the effects of pandemic disease, social disintegration and intertribal warfare, the indigenous inhabitants of Maine emerged from the first half of the seventeenth century to find themselves besieged by the effects of exploitative trade and the pressures of relentless land acquisition by ever-increasing numbers of European settlers. The result was decades of nearly endless conflict and violence. As one historian of the period sardonically commented, "Every once and awhile peace broke out" on the Maine frontier. It is impossible to estimate the number of lives lost or calculate the effects of suffering endured by the people of Maine during the darkest period of the region's history. What began as an inquiry based on historic curiosity evolved into an eye-opening journey that has become this book.

Admittedly, this is not a definitive work on the French and Indian Wars in Maine. The focus of this book is on the midcoast region from the eastern portions of Casco Bay to the Penobscot River. The midcoast and Kennebec Valley was the cauldron in which resentment, misunderstanding and tensions between the native people and their white neighbors simmered and boiled over in waves of repeated violence, ultimately engulfing all of Maine. The stories of attacks against the communities and outposts of southern Maine during King Philip's War (1675–78), King William's War (1688–99) and Queen Anne's War (1703–13) could fill the pages of a book in their own right. Likewise, several topics of interest and historical relevance have been omitted in an effort to streamline this narrative. The story of Jean Vincent d'Abbadie de St. Castin or Baron St.-Castin is one such omission. Castin was a French military officer residing at Pentagoet (Castine) offering the Penobscot trade goods, political council and military leadership. Castin assimilated into the culture of the Penobscot people and married the daughter of the powerful sagamore Madockawando. Carrying on the family legacy, Castin the Younger, Baron St.-Castin's son and Madockawando's grandson, later wielded considerable influence among the Penobscot as a military and political leader.

BARON JEAN VINCENT de ST. CASTINE
(*real portrait*)

Baron St.-Castin. Castin was a French military officer, trader and councilor among the Penobscot people. Like many early Acadians, Castin embraced many aspects of the native culture and intermarried with the local population. Castin married the daughter of Madockawando, a chief sagamore of the Penobscot people. *Collections of the Maine Historical Society.*

The role of the Mohawk and the Iroquois Confederacy in the diplomatic exchanges between Massachusetts and the eastern tribes has also been glossed over in this work. Years of bitter warfare between the Iroquois and the Abenaki during the beaver wars resulted in Abenaki submission to the covenant chain, a web of peace understandings among the Iroquois, the English and the Algonquian people of the Northeast. Throughout the period of the French and Indian Wars in Maine, Mohawk and Iroquois delegates regularly met with the eastern tribes on behalf of Massachusetts to remind them of their commitment to the covenant chain and cajole or strong-arm them into submission. Despite their traditional fear of the Iroquois, the Mohawk in particular, the native people of Maine routinely dismissed their entreaties and threats. With no particular stakes in the unfolding situation on the Maine frontier, the Iroquois, believing they had in good faith fulfilled their obligations to Massachusetts under the covenant chain, refrained from taking up the hatchet, as they threatened, against the eastern tribes.

Several topics touched on in this book, but not fully expanded on, are interesting subjects in their own right. The activities of Jesuit missionary Father Sebastian Rale among the native people of the Kennebec have long garnered the attention of historians in the unfolding of Dummer's War in the 1720s. However, Rale was not the only Jesuit missionary providing spiritual and political guidance to the native people in Maine. East of the Kennebec, Fathers Thury, Bigot, Vincent and Lauverjat resided among and gave council to the people of the Penobscot. The mistrust and animosity between the region's Scots-Irish inhabitants and the representatives of the Massachusetts government at St. George is another fascinating aspect of the region's history during the period. As the embodiment of the government's unpopular conciliatory policies toward the resident Penobscot, Captain Jabez Bradbury and his right-hand man, Thomas Fletcher, became the repeated targets of local invectives and accusations. The indictments leveled against these two men reflect the fears, frustrations and cultural predispositions of the region's white inhabitants whose legacy has helped shape the culture and character of midcoast Maine today.

For those looking to delve deeper into this period of Maine history, mountains of material are available to the intrepid researcher and casual historian alike. Tomes of primary source information—including period letters, journals, newspapers and government records—are readily available. A number of secondary sources, including town histories, general histories of Maine and multivolume histories of the French and Indian Wars, were written during the nineteenth and early twentieth centuries. Recent scholarship has focused more narrowly on particular topics relating to the history of early New England, providing insight into the events as they unfolded in Maine during the period. The story of Maine's native people is the most difficult part of the story to reconstruct. With no history of written language, students of the period are confronted with a void of documentary evidence, and what documentation does exist comes from Europeans writing about the native people of Maine. Although correspondence between native representatives and the government of Massachusetts exists, it was ultimately written by the hand of a nonnative interpreter. Fortunately, renewed interest in the story of the region's native people over the past forty years has contributed to the understanding of their history, culture and ethnology. By combining the information available from disparate sources, it is possible to piece together a reasonably clear and fascinating mosaic of Maine's colonial history. I hope this book plants seeds of interest just as Mr. Skoglund's words did for me many years ago.

# Chapter 1

# *Dawnland*

Maine has not always been deserving of its license plate moniker "vacationland." Popular images of quaint harbor villages, scenic seaside vistas and quiet forests belie a dark and troubled past. For a period of nearly eighty years, between 1675 and 1759, Maine was ravaged by a series of six wars pitting fledgling colonies, European powers and indigenous people against one another. Civilians were the primary targets on both sides. Over the course of these conflicts, multiple communities were reduced to ashes or completely abandoned out of fear and the inability to defend themselves. Countless men, women and children were killed or taken into captivity to be sold into servitude or held for ransom. The dead were often stripped of their scalps, which were sold for exorbitant prices as gruesome trophies. Those left behind often found it difficult to sustain themselves over harsh Maine winters as both sides sought to destroy their enemies' crops, livestock and property. This is the ugly history of Maine that has largely been forgotten.

Each of the six conflicts that raged across Maine during the period is referred to by its own distinct yet confusingly similar name: King Philip's War (1675–78), King William's War (1688–99), Queen Anne's War (1703–13), Dummer's War (1721–26), King George's War (1745–49), and the French and Indian War (1755–59).[1] Neatly separating, categorizing and naming these conflicts may be useful when looking through a particular historical lens, such as the conflict between European powers in North America or providing a chronological reference for specific events. However, in considering the broad history of the eastern frontier, it quickly becomes apparent that these conflicts are interrelated continuations of one another and derive their genesis from the animosity that developed between the area's white and native populations. Although at times occurring within the broader framework of the conflict between England and France, the wars carried out on Maine soil were of a decidedly local nature. These were parallel wars waged within the greater context of imperial struggle but with distinctly local and personal goals.[2]

Old-world problems of political and religious conflict continued with the establishment of new-world colonies. In this new geopolitical environment, conflicts between powers in Europe spilled over to their peripheral colonies and vice versa. From the mid-seventeenth to the early nineteenth century, virtually all the European powers were embroiled in conflicts over the balance of power in Europe and overseas expansion. King William's War inaugurated the beginning of armed hostilities between England and France in North America. Known as the Nine Years' War in Europe, the war in Maine dragged on for a total of eleven years. Within four years of the conclusion of King William's War, the War of Austrian Succession would engulf the Northeast in the guise of Queen Anne's War. Thirty-two years of stasis between England and France allowed for the gradual reestablishment of English footholds on the Maine coast in the wake of Queen Anne's War. The period was not free from war, however, as Dummer's War erupted in the early 1720s. Unlike the past two conflicts or the wars that would follow, there was no direct intervention by the governments of England or France, and the contest was strictly limited to the native and white societies of New England. War in Europe would again bring New France and New England into armed conflict with the outbreak of the War of Austrian Succession, or King George's War (1745–48), as the conflict would become known in New England.

Despite years of conflict between England and France in the New World, the unrelenting series of wars produced few changes in the geopolitical landscape of North America. Neither side had the strength or the will to upset the balance of power in Europe over its distant colonial holdings. Unaddressed concerns over boundary issues in North America would, however, propel England, France and, ultimately, all the major powers of Europe into yet another conflict that would have profound implications for the people of North America. The French and Indian War—or the Seven Years' War, as it is known in Europe—was truly the first world war. By the war's conclusion in 1763, fighting had raged across Europe, North America and the Caribbean and had reached Africa, India and the Philippines.

Although the war did not materially change the political structure of Europe, the terms of the peace forced France to cede its vast North American holdings to Great Britain, forever changing the destinies of the continent's people, European and native alike.

Europeans were not the only people caught up in the tide of geopolitical conflict during the seventeenth and eighteenth centuries. In North America, the continent's indigenous people engaged in their own struggle for political, economic, social and territorial equilibrium. Seeking to promote their own best interest, native societies engaged in war, trade and diplomacy with the French, the English and other native societies. The various native societies were not mere bystanders caught between two competing European powers but active participants in the struggle for North America. Significantly, the native people were forced to make these choices of war and diplomacy in the wake of drastic social change and upheaval.

During the early 1600s, native societies from the Penobscot to Cape Cod were shaken to their core by pandemic disease, intertribal warfare and ever-increasing dependence on European trade goods. Maine's indigenous societies endured unimaginable human loss, social uncertainty and political fragmentation while contending with ever-increasing European encroachment on their homelands.

The first of the "virgin soil" epidemics appeared soon after initial contact with European traders in the mid-1500s.[3] Having never previously been exposed to many of the diseases carried by European visitors, the aboriginal people were easy prey to a host of newly introduced microorganisms. The most widespread and deadly pandemic appeared in eastern Maine sometime in 1617. By 1619, it had swept through the native population of the Northeast. It is impossible to provide any firm statistics regarding its impact on the population, but it is widely believed that no less than 75 percent of the region's inhabitants succumbed to the disease.[4] In many cases, those who survived were overwhelmed by the magnitude of the calamity and unable to care for the sick and dying. The dead went unburied, and entire villages were wiped out or abandoned. Traditional rhythms of food procurement were interrupted by the ravages of the disease, causing further hardship for those who survived. Powwows, the traditional healers and spiritual leaders, were powerless in the face of the disease. Society as these people knew it was crumbling before them. In the aftermath of this crisis, the native people of Maine were forced to reassemble the pieces of their social institutions. At the same time, they would encounter continued threats to their security and independence.

The establishment of trade with Europeans profoundly changed the native societies of Maine. Not only did it initially facilitate the spread of deadly pathogens, but the introduction of trade goods also revolutionized the material culture of the native people and the means by which they conducted their daily lives, as well as the ways in which they interacted with their environment and themselves. In the Gulf of Maine region, early trade connections were established between the native population and European explorers and fishermen. Initial contacts likely occurred no later than the early 1500s between Basque fishermen operating off Nova Scotia and the Micmac people who called the area home. In 1524, explorer Giovanni de Verrazano recorded an act of intercultural show-and-tell with Native Americans in the vicinity of Casco Bay.[5] By the early 1600s, the native inhabitants of coastal Maine were in regular and routine contact with both French and English traders and fishermen. Trade provided the cornerstone of the cultural intercourse that transpired on the shores of North America. The Stone Age aboriginal inhabitants exchanged furs and feathers for kettles, textiles, knives, axes, firearms and alcohol. These items were quickly incorporated into the native people's webs of interpersonal relationships, trade and diplomacy.

Long before the introduction of European goods in the sixteenth and seventeenth centuries, trade played a vital role within and between native societies. Trade and gift giving had a long-established tradition among the Algonquin-speaking people of the Northeast. It was through this mechanism, in part, that sagamores, clan leaders and heads of family bands derived the consensus on which their authority to lead rested. Diplomatic efforts between native groups were likewise facilitated by trade and gift giving, and there is evidence of extended trade networks linking distant people and cultures. Trade in this context was more important to the native people for its social, symbolic significance than its economic function. The revolution wrought by the introduction of European goods radically transformed this system of exchange into a quest for material acquisition. Furs and land became commodities to be swapped for the European goods upon which native people were becoming increasingly dependent. The transformation of a people long accustomed to being stewards of their land and its resources to increasingly desperate mortgagers of their independence was well underway by the end of the seventeenth century.

During the first half of the seventeenth century, nearly all of the Northeast's native societies became embroiled in a series of conflicts over access to the natural resource commodities that fueled the trade in

Trade goods. Accompanying the iron scale are typical European trade goods available through Massachusetts's truck house system. The knives and biscuit are representative of what native people could have traded for one beaver skin, on top of which they are displayed. *Courtesy of Ken Hamilton.*

European goods. In southern New England, armed conflict would arise over access to quahog shells that were used to make wampum. In Maine and elsewhere in the Northeast, European demand for beaver pelts propelled the region into a series of conflicts that became known as the Beaver Wars. Coming on the heels of the great pandemic of 1617–19, the Beaver Wars compounded the social and political changes underway among the indigenous people of Maine. As a result of the pandemic and the Beaver Wars, the indigenous people of Maine appear to have experienced a political realignment that shaped their relationships with Europeans and each other for the next 150 years.

Considerable ambiguity exists regarding the ethnic, social and political distinctions of the Northeast's indigenous people. Despite differences among the people of the region, they all shared a similar Algonquin religious and linguistic heritage. They also shared similar ideas of social and political order in which the mantle of leadership was gained through popular consent rather than coercion or unquestioned obedience. The most fundamental unit of social order and polity lay in the kinship band. These kinship bands were free to associate themselves with those leaders whom they felt could best represent their interest and provide for their needs. Kinship bands sharing similar interests and needs would coalesce into a sort of clan structure, and clans would come together to form the basis of what is thought of as the tribe. Although political authority was not derived from familial lineage, leaders often emerged from large and influential families. While the institution of the kinship band survived, there appears to have been a political reorganization of the tribes in the wake of war and disease.

Early European chroniclers of Maine, both French and English, described several strong tribal leaders who appeared to have been vested with centralized tribal authority. French records identified three sociopolitical groups in the Gulf of Maine region.[6] Inhabiting Nova Scotia and New Brunswick to the St. John River was a people identified as the Souriquois. To the west of the Souriquois, the Etchemin occupied the lands between the St. John and Kennebec Rivers, while the Almouchiquois lay claim to the lands south and west of the Kennebec. Although early English observers seem to be slightly more nuanced in their assessment of the ethnic identities of Maine's native population, they fundamentally support the idea of a small number of strong native political entities along the Maine coast. By the second half of the seventeenth century, however, it appears that the eastern tribes had become politically fragmented, with a host of leaders claiming to represent disparate kinship bands.

By the beginning of the eighteenth century, the government of Massachusetts, which was responsible for the administration of Maine, consistently used appellations for native societies based on their place of residence. Although probably imprecise, the nomenclature used by Massachusetts provides broad insight into how the native societies of Maine arranged themselves politically. The Eastern Tribes, as recognized by Massachusetts, consisted of the Cape Sable, St. John, Penobscot, Kennebec, Amarascoggin[7] and Piqwacket Indians. Residing in Nova Scotia and portions of New Brunswick, the Cape Sable Indians were undoubtedly the same people earlier identified as the Souriquois and would later be known as the Micmac. Centered in the St. John River area of eastern Maine and western New Brunswick, the St. John Indians would today be identified as the Passamaquoddy and Malicites and could trace their ethnic identity back to the Etchemin identified by the French. The Penobscot who occupied the land from roughly Mount Desert Island to the St. George River are harder to identify ethnically. While they retained close relations with the St. John people to their east and are often classified in period documents as Tarrentine, they are at other times recognized as eastern Abenaki.[8] To the west of the Penobscot people, the Kennebec or Canibas Indians of the Kennebec River area were at times referred to as Norridgewock Indians in the correspondence of Massachusetts officials. The Kennebec or Norridgewock Indians were Abenaki in ethnic composition and closely related to the Amarascoggin and Piqwacket to their west. Living along the Androscoggin and Saco Rivers, respectively, the Amarascoggin and Piqwacket peoples represented the other Abenaki people of Maine.

Although Massachusetts clearly identified six eastern tribes, in looking at the records of negotiations and treaties, it is readily apparent that by the eighteenth century, none of the tribes possessed any sort of centralized authority. Multiple members of a single tribe invariably affixed their names or totems to a single document, and Massachusetts negotiators regularly made inquiries as to whether representatives were able to speak on behalf of other tribal factions in their absence. An example of the diplomatic difficulties created by the eastern tribes' political factionalism can be seen in an early effort to bring King William's War in Maine to an end. In August 1693, a peace treaty was signed at Pemaquid between Massachusetts and the eastern Indians. Thirteen sagamores representing the Kennebec and Penobscot signed the treaty.[9] Despite this seemingly broad representation, the treaty proved unsatisfactory to native people as a whole, and internal divisions over the sale of land to the English by Madockawando, one of the

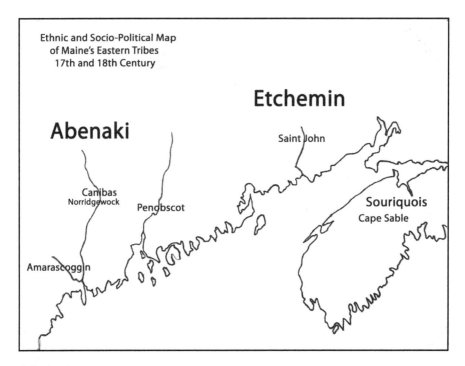

*Author's map.*

Penobscot representatives, led to the rejection of the treaty and six more years of war. Diplomacy between Massachusetts and the eastern tribes would continue to be plagued by the native people's political fragmentation and difficulty achieving consensus. Recurrent instances of splintered and partial commitments from portions of the eastern tribes led Massachusetts to believe that the native people of Maine consistently acted with perfidy and ill faith. Ultimately, this factionalism prevented the native people from effectively advocating for themselves in the face of increasing tension with their English neighbors.

What began as an essentially harmonious relationship between the native people of Maine and European visitors gradually soured as those Europeans made permanent inroads on North America. During the early 1600s, seasonal fishing stations and temporary fur trading outposts began to appear on the rocky shores and navigable rivers of midcoast Maine. Monhegan, Damariscove, Cape Newagen and Pemaquid all served as important temporary fishing outposts for English fishing ventures.

Transient fur trading operations were established by the English at Cushnoc in what is now Augusta and at Pejeepscot, where the Androscoggin

Pemaquid fisherman's house. This reconstructed seventeenth-century building typifies the type of dwelling found at the early Pemaquid fishing station. Fishing stations such as this one dotted the midcoast region at Monhegan, Damariscove and Cape Newagen. Seasonal and later permanent fishing stations helped fuel white settlement of the midcoast region. *Author's photo.*

and Kennebec Rivers meet to form Merrymeeting Bay. Both the French and the English attempted to establish permanent settlements on the Gulf of Maine between 1604 and 1613. At the mouth of the Kennebec River in present Phippsburg, John Popham and his associates attempted to establish the first permanent English settlement in 1607. The project ultimately failed, but it was a portent of English intentions to settle the region. French endeavors to launch settlements at the mouth of the St. Croix River in 1604 and Mount Desert Island in 1613 likewise failed, but failure was only temporary. By the late 1620s, the English had established themselves at Pemaquid, and by 1635, the French were entrenched at Pentagoet in today's Castine. By 1675, English communities dotted the coast of Maine from the Piscataqua to the Damariscotta River. Increased European presence in the former homelands of Maine's native people ultimately led to misunderstanding and increased tension, eventually resulting in eighty years of war.

The issues dividing the native and European people of Maine arose from five basic and often intertwined points of contention. Divergent notions of land, trade, language, sovereignty and justice all contributed to the misunderstanding and mistrust that characterized native and European relations during the seventeenth and eighteenth centuries. The sale, ownership and use of land became increasingly problematic as English settlers permanently established themselves and sought to acquire more land for their rapidly expanding population. The growing dependency of the indigenous people on European trade goods and the resulting interactions between societies periodically engendered frustration and desperation among Maine's native people and helped fuel land controversy. Misunderstandings in the application of language and covenants led to divergent views regarding transactions and agreements, which often resulted in failed expectations for both sides. English views of native polity and sovereignty also undermined hopes for stability and peaceful coexistence in the province of Maine.[10] Finally, native inability to achieve satisfactory justice through the English legal system wrought frustration and suspicion between the two cultures.

Astonishing growth of the white population in America during the seventeenth and eighteenth centuries fueled English appropriation of native lands. From the time of initial settlement in the early 1600s to 1750, the population of the English colonies in America ballooned to approximately two million people. In Maine, the white population had reached an estimated six thousand people on the eve of King Philip's War in 1675 and more than fifteen thousand by the time the last frontier war, the French and Indian War, erupted in 1755.[11] Irrespective of the aboriginal population that already resided in and laid claim to the lands of Maine, the English Crown, through the agency of the Council of Plymouth, awarded large tracts of land to several well-connected individuals and corporations. Grantees were expected to settle and develop these grants for their own, and by extension the Crown's, economic benefit. During the 1620s and early 1630s, the midcoast region from Brunswick, up the Kennebec valley and eastward to the St. George River was parceled out in four grants: the Pejeepscot, Plymouth, Pemaquid and Muscongus patents. In time, each of these entities would seek to capitalize on its holdings through the introduction of permanent settlers who would improve the land and build infrastructure. Throughout the seventeenth century, these grants remained largely inactive. Indian deeds, which overlapped the grants made by the Council of Plymouth, fueled the initial settlement of Maine. These Indian deeds were procured through the direct sale of land by native sagamores to individual and small party interests. Although the native people of Maine attempted to accommodate the influx of white settlers through the sale of lands and negotiations delineating the bounds of English expansion, persistent English disregard for territorial limits repeatedly led to confrontations along the frontier of Maine. Native remonstrances were frequently met with indifference, hollow platitudes and defensiveness, thus further dividing the people who called Maine home.

Initially, trade between the native people and Europeans was a symbiotic exchange. Native people desired European goods, including tools, textiles and firearms; Europeans wanted furs and access to land. Quickly, native people found themselves in an ever-increasing state of dependency on these goods, as they had revolutionized the way in which native people lived. Increasing demand for these goods, coupled with decreasing resources with which to conduct trade, created frustration and a sense of desperation. Native people complained of predatory practices by English traders, who frequently conducted trade with the assistance of alcohol and who seemingly sought ever-increasing prices for goods while devaluing those commodities that natives offered in exchange. Although this undoubtedly provoked mistrust and animosity, it did not in and of itself lead directly to armed conflict. Paradoxically, periodic English suspension of the firearms trade due to concerns over native uprisings did propel the native people of Maine into war with their white neighbors. By the time of King Philip's War, the native people of Maine had abandoned the use of flaked projectile points and had become wholly reliant on European firearms, gunpowder and lead shot for their traditional practice of hunting. Without the ability to trade for these items, the native people faced the very real possibility of not being able to provide for their own sustenance. They were therefore faced with four terrible alternatives: watch their families starve; surrender themselves totally and completely to English control; leave their homelands and live among the French in Canada; or wage war in the hopes of forcing some sort of negotiated peace and the resumption of trade.

Mistrust and misunderstanding between the native people of Maine and their English neighbors was also exacerbated by differences in language and culture. Negotiations between native and white parties were invariably conducted in the English language, facilitated by both native, French and English translators. Discrepancies in the understanding of these proceedings frequently undermined relations between the two cultures. These discrepancies can be attributed to lost nuances in language as well as deliberate misrepresentation by the translators themselves. Further complicating relations, treaties, deeds and other binding agreements were, according to European tradition, committed to writing as a contract in perpetuity. This was a foreign notion to the native people of Maine, who had no heritage of written language and who viewed oral covenants as binding only so long as the subscribers possessed authority to enforce them. As a result, both sides frequently believed that the other acted in ill faith, leading to social and political apprehensions that undermined the possibility of long-term peaceful coexistence in Maine.

English failure to accept and understand the sovereignty of the region's native people likewise proved a barrier to peaceful relations in Maine. Both English and French records of the period frequently refer to the native people as "savages," people living in a state of nature without the same social institutions of church and state that marked European civility. In the context of the European mind, these people could not be sovereign in their own right. Rather, both the English and the French viewed the native people as children in need of tutelage, vassals in their imperial designs. As a condition of peace and diplomacy, both the English and French repeatedly demanded that the various native peoples of Maine accept their respective monarch as their supreme sovereign power. Throughout the period, the native people walked this tightrope of French and English demands with varying degrees of success. Certainly the native people attempted to play the English and the French to their own best advantage. While the eastern tribes generally attempted to pursue a policy of neutrality, internal factionalism and forces beyond their control ultimately propelled them into war with their white neighbors.

Conflicting notions of justice also impeded relations between the native people of Maine and their English neighbors. Traditional native concepts of compensatory justice, in which serious transgressions could be assuaged through gift giving or retaliation, were at odds with English customs of due process and trial by jury. By treaty provisions established in the wake of war, Maine's native people agreed to settle grievances with the English through courts of law rather than acts of retribution. However, native attempts to achieve satisfaction through the English legal system proved futile and frustrating. This perceived travesty of justice would, in combination with other inflammatory factors, lead to the unraveling of peaceful coexistence on the Maine frontier.

## Chapter 2

# *Two Kings*

Most historians agree that King Philip's War in Maine was only tangentially related to the war that devastated Rhode Island and Massachusetts to the south. Like subsequent wars fought on Maine soil between white and native inhabitants, King Philip's War in Maine was the result of and characterized by local issues and concerns, occurring within the context of a broader struggle. King Philip's War, so named for the native sagamore who assumed leadership of the uprising in Massachusetts and Rhode Island, erupted in late June 1675 when a band of Pokanoket looted and set fire to several English homes in Swansea, Massachusetts.[12] The situation quickly escalated, plunging the Northeast into the most costly war in American history.[13] Although the war in southern New England would come to a close by August 1676, the conflict in Maine would continue until 1678.

Alarmed by the outbreak of hostilities to the south and fearful of spreading unrest, Massachusetts banned the sale of firearms, shot and gunpowder to the eastern tribes while demanding the native people surrender all firearms already in their possession. These measures caused considerable consternation among the native inhabitants of Maine, who had become reliant on the use of firearms for the procurement of game to feed their people. Prior to 1654, Maine's native people had been able to obtain trade items, including firearms, through both French and English sources. However, the English seizure and destruction of the French trading post at Pentagoet at the mouth of the Penobscot River effectively eliminated the French from the web of trade from Penobscot Bay southward, forcing the native people into dependence on the English. Aside from the immediate subsistence crises created by the curtailment of the firearms trade, the proposed seizure of native weapons was seen as an affront to the autonomy of the native people. While some native factions sought peace and accommodation with their English neighbors by relinquishing their firearms, others patently refused. The situation on the Maine frontier was further complicated during the summer of 1675 by the wanton killing of Sagamore Squando's infant son, who was cast into the Saco River by a band of English sailors curious whether native children could naturally swim.

The opening salvo of King Philip's War in Maine occurred on September 5, 1675, when the home of Thomas Purchase was looted by a band of natives who approached the house under the pretense of trade. The exact location of Purchase's house has been lost to time, but it was likely located near the falls of the Androscoggin River in present Brunswick.[14] Purchase arrived in the area no later than 1628 and soon established himself as a farmer and trader of questionable repute among the natives with whom he had dealings. This likely explains why Purchase and his house became a particular target at the beginning of the war. Within days of the attack against the Purchase house, the family of Thomas Wakely was assaulted at their home in what is now Portland. It is unclear why the Wakelys were chosen as the war's next victims; perhaps their isolated homestead simply provided a target of opportunity. Regardless of the motives, the nature of the attack was characteristic of how war on the Maine frontier would be conducted for the next eighty years. William Hubbard described the aftermath of the Wakely incident in vivid detail: "The house burned to ashes, the bodies of the old man and his wife half consumed with the fire, the young woman killed, and three of the grandchildren having their brains dashed out...one girl of about eleven years old was carried captive by them."[15]

Other attacks were carried out across Maine throughout the fall and winter of 1675 and 1676. At the head of the New Meadows River, a party of English soldiers was attacked and routed, while the communities of Casco (Greater Portland), Peaks Island, Saco and Kittery all came under attack.

Over the winter of 1675–76, a tentative peace was established in Maine between Massachusetts and the eastern tribes.[16] Desiring the resumption of trade to prevent famine, native representatives agreed to submit themselves to English sovereignty and return all captives they had seized over the past several months. Ultimately, resentment toward and suspicion of the native population by English residents of the midcoast area would undo Maine's fragile peace. Seeking justice for the deaths of their fellow Englishmen, a general warrant was issued for the arrest of native individuals suspected of having taken part in what the English deemed murders committed during the war. Under the guise of the warrant, many Maine natives were seized to stand trial before English courts or be sold into slavery in the West Indies. Ignoring the peace, the residents of Monhegan promoted the continuation of the war by offering a five-pound cash reward for the taking and delivery of any native head. Even the Penobscot, who had so far remained largely neutral, understood that peaceful relations could not be sustained under such conditions, and war resumed during the summer of 1676.

Just as the war was coming to a conclusion in southern New England, a fresh round of violence erupted along midcoast Maine. On August 13, 1676, the trading post of Richard Hammond in what is now Days Ferry in Woolwich fell under attack by a band of native warriors. Like Thomas Purchase, Hammond was a trader believed to have cheated and mistreated his native customers. Hammond and two other men were killed during the attack, and sixteen others were taken captive. The next day, August 14, 1676, the fortified trading post of the Clarke and Lake Company at Arrowsic fell to what was probably the same war party. Perhaps as many as thirty-five people were killed or captured as a result of the attack, while approximately a dozen people escaped to the safety of the off-shore islands.[17] Panic gripped the eastern settlements of the midcoast. The residents of Sheepscot—which encompassed today's village of Sheepscot, Edgecomb, parts of Boothbay, Boothbay Harbor and Westport Island—fled down the Sheepscot River to Cape Newagen at the tip of Southport Island, leaving behind all their worldly possessions, including more than four hundred head of cattle. The residents of Pemaquid likewise fled for fear of their lives. Initially attempting to reach Monhegan, they were stymied by contrary winds and forced to make their way to Damariscove Island off what is now Boothbay. Those from Cape Newagen, as well as individuals from Arrowsic and Casco Bay, soon joined those already seeking shelter on Damariscove. By the middle of August, the island was home to an estimated three hundred English war refugees.[18] From this vantage point, several nautical miles off the coast, displaced English settlers watched the landward sky fill with smoke and flames as their homes and farms were systematically burned by vengeful native warriors. Unable to adequately support and defend themselves on Damariscove, the English exiles of midcoast Maine soon made their way westward to Massachusetts and the Piscataqua River.

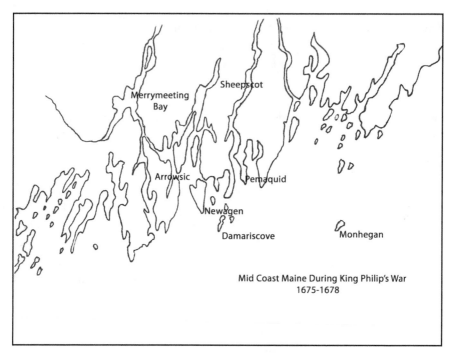

*Author's map.*

In response to the forced abandonment of the eastern settlements, a military expedition under the command of Major Richard Waldron was organized in February 1676/77. The expedition consisted of 150 men from Massachusetts, including many who had been forced from their homes in Maine, and 60 allied Indians from Natick.[19] Prior to the war, Waldron had been a trader with a reputation for unscrupulous dealing with the natives. In September 1676, Waldron lured a group of nearly 200 natives into captivity and slavery in the West Indies when he invited them to what they believed was a peace negotiation at Cocheco (Dover), New Hampshire. Having dubiously earned regard as an Indian fighter, Massachusetts believed that Waldron was the right man to subdue the eastern tribes. With Waldron at its head, the expedition set sail with the goal of reclaiming the eastern settlements and forcing the region's native people into submission.

With the exception of further exacerbating tensions on the Maine frontier, Waldron's expedition accomplished little. Coming ashore at Mere Point in Brunswick on February 18, 1676/77, the expedition proceeded to the confluence of the Androscoggin and Kennebec Rivers in the vicinity of Merrymeeting Bay. There, Waldron established contact with several

Abenaki sagamores of the Amarascoggin and Canibas people, including the Sagamore Squando. Both sides agreed to a parley for peace the next day with the understanding that the Abenaki would deliver any captives in their possession. When the Abenaki returned the next day without their captives, the negotiations degenerated into an exchange of musket fire, forcing Waldron and his men to withdraw. Failure to subdue the Abenaki of the Kennebec and Androscoggin induced Waldron to shift his attention eastward. On February 26, Waldron made arrangements for a conference with a mixed group of natives, including representatives from the Penobscot at Pemaquid. Again, negotiations devolved into armed confrontation, resulting in the death of the venerable Sagamore Mattahondo and ten other Penobscot. Four other native attendees were taken captive during the affair, including Sagamore Madockawando's sister. Having failed to secure the release of a single English captive, Waldron returned to Boston in March. Rather than subduing the eastern tribes, his exploits managed to turn even peace-seeking factions of the Penobscot into ardent supporters of the war.

Widespread, intense attacks against the communities of southern Maine commenced in April 1677 and continued over the summer. Despite the severity of the attacks and the losses incurred, the remaining settlements south of Casco Bay endured. The abandonment of the midcoast, Massachusetts's inability to reclaim the region and the increasingly hostile attitudes of the native people east of the Kennebec prompted concerns that the French might capitalize on the region's instability, asserting their claims to the midcoast as part of Acadia. To secure the region for the English Crown, Governor Edmond Andros of New York dispatched four sloops laden with military stores and soldiers for Pemaquid in June 1677. Upon landing, the New Yorkers began construction of Fort Charles, a wooden structure mounting seven cannon with a garrison of fifty men. Struck by this show of military force, the Penobscot, weary of war and desperately desiring the resumption of trade, began extending peace overtures in August 1677. By the end of the year, the other eastern tribes likewise sought to conclude this disastrous, inconclusive war.

In April 1678, representatives of the eastern tribes and Massachusetts successfully negotiated an end to the conflict with the Treaty of Casco. Neither side emerged from the conflict with a decided advantage; both sides were exhausted and desperately wanted to end the hostilities. With the exception of a few conciliatory provisions, the treaty largely affirmed the status quo as it had existed prior to the war. The most lasting and significant result of the Treaty of Casco was the native people's agreement to allow English reoccupation of those areas settled prior to the outbreak of the war.[20]

Over the next decade, English settlers reoccupied the Maine coast from Casco Bay to Pemaquid. Although the Treaty of Casco brought a halt to the fighting in Maine, it did little to address the real grievances fostering the divide between natives and whites. While Maine's native people continued to express dissatisfaction with the practices of English traders in the region, land-related issues took the forefront in fomenting tension along the Maine frontier. Following King Philip's War, the English not only reclaimed their former settlements but in short order also began to expand their presence through the acquisition of more native land. English land use practices also contributed to the growing disaffection between the native and white populations of Maine. In areas where native people engaged in agricultural pursuits, particularly in southern Maine, free-ranging English livestock frequently destroyed native crops, while the English use of fish seines and the construction of dams at mill sites impeded traditional native fishing practices by preventing fish migration. The region's native people made repeated remonstrances to English magistrates concerning the encroachment of English settlers on their lands and the disastrous impact their land use practices were having on their food resources, but to no avail.

Festering tensions came to a head and erupted in open hostility during the summer of 1688. Near Saco, local natives killed several English cattle that had recently destroyed their crops. In response, English officials seized twenty native hostages to be exchanged for the individuals responsible for the destruction of settlers' livestock. Reacting to the seizure of hostages at Saco and English encroachment on native lands in the midcoast, North Yarmouth (Yarmouth, Freeport and Harpswell) was attacked, leaving several soldiers working on a nearby garrison dead. The attack prompted thirty-six families residing in the area to abandon their homes, leaving them to be burned by the Indians. At Merrymeeting Bay, nine people were taken captive and several subsequently killed. Attacks against Newcastle and Sheepscot resulted in several families being taken captive and the destruction of the settlements. In response, Governor Andros issued a proclamation ordering the offending natives to surrender all English captives and to hand over for trial all individuals guilty of committing murder during these attacks. Andros's proclamation was perceived as tantamount to a declaration of war, and the Maine frontier was again engulfed in violence.

King William's War, as this war came to be known, dragged on for more than a decade in Maine, and the local conflict would be subsumed as part of the greater contest between England and France. Within a year of the war's outbreak, all the English settlements east of Wells were abandoned in the face of intense, large-scale native attacks. The midcoast region, Pemaquid in particular, became ground zero in the struggle among England, France and the eastern tribes. During the course of the war, the French and the eastern tribes used each other for their own mutual benefit. French support provided the eastern tribes access to goods including food supplies and weapons, allowing them to prosecute the war in a way they had been unable to do during King Philip's War. Ties with the French also provided the eastern tribes with a strong ally who, like themselves, desired to push the English out of vast areas of Maine.

The French had maintained an interest in the coast of Maine—Acadia, as they called it—from the beginning of the seventeenth century. The Treaty of Breda, which ended hostilities among the English, French and Dutch in 1677, confirmed French claims to the region but failed to establish Acadia's precise boundaries. While the French asserted dominion over the Maine coast as far west as the Kennebec, the English claimed sovereignty over the same land as far east as the St. Croix River. This dispute continued to be a source of contention between France and England in North America for the next seventy-five years. However, England and France were not the only powers vying for control of this region. Caught between the imperial ambitions of England and France, the indigenous people of Maine's eastern tribes sought to assert their own sovereignty and independence, conducting war, peace, trade and diplomacy in their own best interest. Whereas King Philip's War had strictly been a contest between the English and the native people of Maine, the advent of King William's War inaugurated the beginning of a prolonged and multifaceted contest for the coast of Maine.

Occupying the crossroads of the English, French and native worlds in Maine, Pemaquid became an important strategic and symbolic site for all the warring parties. Fort Charles, which was established as a bulwark against French aspirations in Maine in 1677, still stood in 1689. The area had been reoccupied by English settlers following King Philip's War, and the site was reestablished as a trading center shortly after the founding of the fort. By the outbreak of King William's War in 1689, Pemaquid was the easternmost settlement, military post and trading outpost in British North America. As such, the fort and community at Pemaquid straddled the front lines of the war sweeping across the coast of Maine.

Over the summer of 1689, the people of the eastern tribes orchestrated an attempt to dislodge the English from Pemaquid and the midcoast.

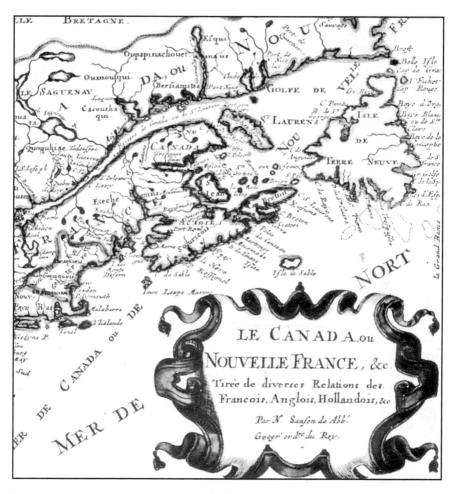

This period map of New France and New England shows French Acadia extending as far south as the Kennebec River. Conflicting English and French claims to the territory between the Kennebec and St. Croix Rivers contributed to the instability and turmoil in Maine during the late seventeenth and early eighteenth centuries. *Courtesy of Wikimedia Commons.*

The native attack against Pemaquid on August 2 took the community's residents and fort's complement completely by surprise. The expedition to take the fort departed from Penobscot by canoe, landing in what is today Round Pond. The party of between one and two hundred Indians made their way several miles overland and positioned themselves between the fort and the settlement to prevent the inhabitants from reaching the safety of the stockade.[21] Although some of the inhabitants were able to make their way into the fort, many more were seized and taken captive. Fighting

36

between the garrison and the assaulting natives continued throughout the day and into the night. Using abandoned cellars and a large rock formation immediately to the west of the fort as cover, the natives were able to apply enough pressure for Lieutenant Weems, the fort's commander, to seek terms of capitulation the following day. Under the terms of surrender, what remained of the fort's garrison and those inhabitants who sought shelter there were allowed to depart Pemaquid for Boston with whatever they could carry in their hands. Those inhabitants who failed to reach the safety of the fort did not share the same fortunate fate as those who departed for Boston with Lieutenant Weems and the garrison. Perhaps as many as fifty men, women and children, including nine-year-old John Gyles, were taken back to Penobscot as captives.[22]

The fall of Fort Charles at Pemaquid occasioned the complete abandonment of the midcoast settlements east of Casco (Portland). In late September, Casco came under attack by a sizable native war party that was beaten back by the timely arrival of 250 men, including native allies under the command of Benjamin Church, who had earned notoriety as an Indian fighter during King Philip's War. Having prevented the fall of Casco, Church proceeded to range the Maine coast as far as Pemaquid. Failing to encounter any native people in his search-and-destroy mission, Church and his men returned to Boston before the onset of winter.

On May 25, 1690, a mixed force of French Canadians and native warriors from the Kennebec and Penobscot numbering between four and five hundred returned to Casco to take the now easternmost bastion known as Fort Loyal.[23] Luring a large contingent of the garrison into an ambush, the war party fell upon and destroyed the village. Besieging the fort for four days, the attackers dug a trench from a nearby ravine up to the fort's palisade, allowing them to throw hand grenades over the walls and place a barrel of combustible tar in preparation to consume the fort in fire. Facing an untenable position, the fort's commander, Sylvanus Davis, reached out to the French commander to seek terms of capitulation. Believing he had arranged for the safety of his garrison and the townspeople who had sought refuge in the fort, Davis surrendered. Rather than being given safe passage to the closest English town, as Davis expected, the survivors of the French and Indian attack were committed to captivity. The loss of Fort Loyal and the community at Casco (Portland) further reduced the English footprint in Maine to four communities extending no farther east than Wells.

Despite the loss of the eastern settlements, Massachusetts continued to send military expeditions into the midcoast region on a regular basis. In

September 1690, Major Benjamin Church returned to the coast of Maine, landing at Maquoit (Brunswick/Freeport) with a force of three hundred provincial soldiers. Overnight, Church's force marched to the site of abandoned Fort Andros on the lower falls of the Androscoggin. Surprising a band of natives who occupied the fort, Church's force liberated a handful of English captives and took several native women and children—who later proved to be the wives and family of local native leaders—captive. From Fort Andros, the provincial expedition ascended the Androscoggin River approximately forty miles to a fortified native village located at the upper falls of the river. Church attacked and overtook the village, killing twenty-one natives and recovering seven English captives.[24] After looting and burning the village, Church returned to Maquoit and reembarked his troops and captives for Winter Harbor (Saco).

By 1690, war between England and France for the control of Acadia had begun to intensify. Sir William Phips, recently returned from England with a knighthood and a crown appointment as provost marshal general, would lead the charge. Phips was born in Arrowsic (Woolwich), overlooking the Sheepscot River. As a young man, he was apprenticed to a Boston shipbuilder. Upon the completion of his apprenticeship, he returned to Arrowsic, where he engaged in shipbuilding until he was forced to leave in the midst of King Philip's War. Resuming his shipbuilding trade in Boston, Phips was soon drawn to the sea in search of Spanish treasure. Phips's success

Sir William Phips, shipwright, treasure hunter, soldier, diplomat and the first royal governor of Massachusetts. Phips's land deal with Sagamore Madockawando undermined prospects for peace in 1693. The land Phips obtained in this deal would later filter through the hands of Samuel Waldo and later Henry Knox. *Private collection.*

as a treasure hunter earned him a coveted knighthood and a strong network of influential patronage. Returning to Massachusetts in the midst of war, Phips was charged with breaking the French hold on the Gulf of Maine.

Leaving Boston with seven ships and approximately 500 men, Phips arrived off the Acadian capital of Port Royal on May 11, 1690.[25] Not only was Port Royal the government center of Acadia, but it was also an important port through which the French received supplies destined for distribution to eastern tribes. After taking and looting Port Royal, Phips dispatched his ships to seize other French ports along the Bay of Fundy in an effort to further disrupt the activities of French privateers and the flow of supplies to the native people of Maine. Upon his return to Boston, Phips found preparations underway for a seaborne expedition against the city of Quebec. In August, the fleet and 2,200 provincial soldiers under the command of Phips set sail for the St. Lawrence River.[26] Arriving at Quebec in early October, the naval force expended its meager supply of ammunition bombarding the city's walls while the land force deployed to the east of the city remained inactive due to cold, smallpox and a shortage of supplies. A well-conceived but poorly executed attack by the land forces and Phips's naval squadron ended in disaster, forcing the abandonment of the expedition. After only ten days in front of Quebec's walls, Phips and his defeated force withdrew up the St. Lawrence and returned to Massachusetts.

In 1691, Massachusetts again organized an expedition to range the Maine coast as far as Pejeepscot (Brunswick). In September, four companies under the overall command of John March disembarked at Maquoit to scour the area for native men, women and children. Failing to encounter their intended prey, March and his soldiers returned to their transports in Maquoit Bay. As the men were boarding the transports, they came under attack by a native war party lying in wait. Captain Samuel Sherburne—who commanded one of the four companies—and several soldiers were killed in the opening volleys of the attack. In the chaos of the ensuing firefight, March was able to get his surviving men aboard their vessels. However, an unfavorable tide kept the ships close to shore, and the exchange of fire continued on both sides until the tide turned, allowing the ships to slip down the bay and out of danger.

With the abandonment of the eastern communities, the eastern tribes turned their attention to the remaining English communities of southern Maine. At daybreak on January 24, 1691/92, a force of approximately three hundred native warriors led in part by Penobscot sagamore Madockawando descended on the unprepared village of York. With the sounding of a signal gun, native parties simultaneously fanned out across the community, breaking into homes, killing and scalping the occupants and then setting fire to the houses. By the end of the attack, all that remained of the town were the four garrison houses providing shelter to those fortunate enough to escape the initial onslaught. Perhaps as many as seventy-five people were killed during the raid, with still others being carried into captivity.[27] Effectively isolated following the reduction of York, Wells was attacked by a force of four hundred natives led by Madockawando, Egeremet and Moxus along with a small French contingent in early June. Despite overwhelming odds, the community's defensible position at Storer's Garrison, supported by two armed sloops anchored in the harbor, held off the native assailants for nearly forty-eight hours. Having exhausted their supply of ammunition, the native war party killed the only captive taken during the raid and withdrew.

In the spring of 1692, Sir William Phips received a commission as the first royal governor of Massachusetts from the English Crown, along with orders to reestablish a fort at Pemaquid. In early August, Phips and 450 men under the command of Benjamin Church set sail from Boston. Leaving part of his force behind to complete construction of the fort at Pemaquid, Church proceeded to range Penobscot Bay and the Kennebec River, resulting in the destruction of native food stores and the native village at Taconnet (Winslow). When the fort was completed, it boasted an impressive façade and an even more impressive price tag. The fort is estimated to have cost £20,000, nearly two-thirds the annual budget of the already cash-strapped Massachusetts Bay Colony.[28] Built of stone with a twenty-nine-foot-tall round bastion, walls at least six feet thick and mounting between fourteen and eighteen cannon,[29] Fort William Henry, as the structure was called, presented a truly formidable obstacle to French designs on lower Acadia. It also represented a renewed English threat to the native people of eastern Maine.

As Fort William Henry was being built, Madockawando and several other sagamores from the eastern tribes traveled to Quebec beseeching the French for additional aid. The French agreed to organize an expedition with two warships which, with the aid of the eastern tribes, would range the Maine coast. The expected warships arrived off Penobscot in the fall of 1692 and proceeded westward to Pemaquid. Encountering Fort William Henry and an English warship riding at anchor in the harbor, the French, unprepared for such a confrontation and experiencing unfavorable weather conditions, withdrew from the waters of Maine, leaving the eastern tribes confused and frustrated. Having lost several important sagamores, feeling abandoned by the French and experiencing food shortages caused by the disruptions of

Fort William Henry, Pemaquid. Built in 1692, the fort's walls would have reached nearly to the top of the reconstructed southwest bastion. The site was occupied by two other forts, Fort Charles and Fort Frederick. In 1696, Fort William Henry was besieged and taken by a mixed force of French and Indians. *Author's photo.*

war, native representatives from the various eastern tribes reached out to Governor Phips of Massachusetts in hopes of reestablishing peace, trade and the return of their people being held captive.

In early August 1693, representatives of Massachusetts, including Governor Phips, met with delegates of the eastern tribes at Pemaquid to conduct peace negotiations. On August 12, thirteen sagamores and chief captains representing the native people of the Saco, Androscoggin, Kennebec and Penobscot Rivers signed or placed their totems on a written peace treaty. In signing the treaty, the native representatives—including Madockawando and Edgermet—renounced ties to the French while proclaiming "hearty subjection and obedience unto the Crown of England."[30] The treaty stipulated that the eastern tribes cease all hostilities with the English, release all English captives without ransom, settle disputes through English courts rather than through armed conflict and recognize English land claims. With the exception of an agreement to resume trade, no binding expectations were placed on the English according to the terms of the treaty. Although signed by leading sagamores of the eastern tribes, the treaty was widely rejected by the native people as a whole because of its decidedly English bias. Acceptance of the treaty was further undermined when it was learned that Madockawando, despite questionable authority to do so, had sold a large parcel of land to Sir William Phips in the area now encompassing Thomaston, Warren and Cushing. Despite the prospect of peace kindled by the signing of the agreement, war persisted as attacks were soon renewed against the settlements of southern Maine.

The rhythm of war continued along the Maine coast for the next two years. The ravages of disease and hunger prompted native leaders to seek negotiations several times during 1694 and 1695, but the prospect of peace was dashed on every occasion by mistrust and periodic violence. In the late spring of 1696, the French renewed their designs on lower Acadia in a manner reminiscent of the failed 1692 sortie. Departing Quebec with several warships and eighty French and Canadian soldiers, Pierre Le Moyne d'Iberville set sail for the Maine coast. By the time he reached Penobscot, Iberville had been joined by additional Canadians and several hundred Micmac, St. John and Penobscot warriors. With Fort William Henry in his sights, Iberville, with his mixed armada of French warships and Indian canoes, moved down Penobscot Bay, landing at what is now New Harbor.

From New Harbor, Iberville sent cannons and mortars overland with his mixed force of French and Indians while he moved his warships into the outer harbor of Pemaquid in front of the fort. By the afternoon of the following day, the French had Fort William Henry surrounded and began lobbing mortar shells over the fort's walls. Mounting fifteen cannon and with a garrison of ninety-five well-supplied men, the fort should have been able to withstand a prolonged siege. However, the fort's position soon became untenable. The fort had not been designed to withstand an attack from its landward side, and inexplicably, the garrison's sole source of water was a well located outside the fort's walls. The fort itself had been poorly built, and the stonework began to crumble under the concussive force of the fort's own guns. After offering token resistance, Pasco Chubb, the English commander, accepted the terms of surrender offered by Iberville and turned Fort William Henry over to the French and Indians. Seizing the fort's cannons for themselves, the French distributed the muskets, powder and lead shot to their Indians allies. Before returning to their respective places of residence, the French and Indians demolished Fort William Henry, leaving nothing behind but rubble.

Although the destruction of Fort William Henry represented an important symbolic victory for the French and the eastern tribes, it did little to change the strategic situation on the coast of Maine. Within a month of the fort's surrender, Benjamin Church was again leading an expedition against the eastern tribes, destroying crops and disrupting coastal food procurement from the Penobscot River to the Bay of Fundy. A proposed large-scale attack against New England by the French failed to materialize in 1697. Instead, Massachusetts once more brought the war to the front door of the eastern tribes. That summer, John March bolstered garrisons and ranged the Maine coast with a force of five hundred Massachusetts provincial soldiers.

In December 1697, news reached Boston of the Treaty of Ryswick, concluding war between England and France. For the next year, the Maine frontier remained relatively quiet, although no peace was formally established between Massachusetts and the eastern tribes. No longer receiving aid from the French and still under an English trade embargo, the native people of Maine were desperate for peace by the end of the year. In early January 1699, representatives of Massachusetts and the native people of the Penobscot, Kennebec, Androscoggin and Saco Rivers met at Mere Point in present Brunswick to discuss terms of peace. On January 8, the parties signed a treaty essentially restating the conditions of the peace brokered at Pemaquid six years earlier.

Although peace returned to Maine, the root causes of the conflict still remained unresolved. The Treaty of Ryswick returned the political boundaries of North America to their prewar positions without further clarification. In Maine, France still claimed territory as far south as the Kennebec River as part of Acadia, while England asserted dominion over the same land as far eastward as the St. Croix River. In 1693, the peace signed at Pemaquid had been furiously rejected by the native people of Maine. By 1699, the same people were so desperate for an end to hostility and the resumption of trade that they offered little protest to the humiliating conditions of peace. Concerns over land, fair trade and justice before the law remained unaddressed and continued to breed tension between the white and native people of Maine. Unsurprisingly, peace under these conditions proved to be fleeting, and the region would again erupt in violence less than four years later.

# Chapter 3

## *Missions and Mourning*

K ing William's War devastated the communities of Maine, both English and native alike. By the time peace was established at Mere Point in 1699, the English footprint on the coast of Maine had been reduced to the towns of Kittery, York, Wells and the offshore community of Appledore (Isle of Shoals). More than 10 percent of Maine's white population became casualties of war,[31] as upward of 450 people are thought to have lost their lives, while another 250 were seized as captives, some of whom never returned to their homes and families.[32] The war had been equally unkind to the native people. It is impossible to estimate how many lost their lives at the hands of their white neighbors or perished as a result of famine and disease. Although the lands east of Wells had been reclaimed from the English and promises of trade secured, prospects for the future of Maine's native people appeared bleak. Uncertain of what lay ahead, many uprooted themselves and their families, seeking safety and security in the French mission villages of St. Francis (Odanak) and Becancour (Wowenak) along the St. Lawrence River.

Catholic missionary efforts accompanied French colonial endeavors from the early seventeenth century onward. Evidence of Jesuit missionaries visiting the Kennebec Abenaki exists as early as 1611, and by 1613, Jesuit missionaries were attempting to establish a permanent mission on Mount Desert Island known as St. Sauveur.[33] The native people of Maine readily accepted the proselytizing efforts of these French missionaries, and by the 1640s, French priests from both the Jesuit and Capuchin orders were living among them. By the 1670s, the Capuchin order had been entirely supplanted by the Jesuits on the coast of Maine, and permanent Jesuit missions were established among the Kennebec by Gabrielle Druillettes and the Penobscot by Jean Morain. Not only did the Jesuit missionaries provide spiritual guidance for their native parishioners, but they also offered political council and served as conduits to the government of New France and, by extension, the material goods on which the native people depended. Although Jesuit missionaries provided services within the native villages of Maine, further efforts to administer to the spiritual and physical needs of the Algonquin people were underway in Canada.

During the 1630s, Catholic missionaries began establishing communities along the St. Lawrence River between Montreal and Quebec to provide sanctuary and religious evangelism for an influx of Algonquian refugees seeking shelter from the ravages of war with the Iroquois. By the time of King Philip's War in the 1670s, the mission villages had become refuges not only for western Algonquian such as the Huron but also eastern Algonquian from the Amarascoggin, Kennebec and Penobscot people seeking respite from the hardships occasioned by war in Maine. As refugee communities, the mission villages of New France were polyglot communities of mixed tribes and kinship bands who shared similar yet distinct cultural traits. As the mission villages grew in number and evolved over the course of the late seventeenth and early eighteenth centuries, each of the villages developed its own cultural identity and attracted others of the same cultural background.

Emigration from Maine to the Canadian mission villages commenced with the first outbreak of violence during King Philip's War. Initially, those leaving Maine fled to the village of Sillery, the first of the mission villages, which was established in 1634. By the time of King William's War, Sillery had ceased to exist, and the mission village at St. Francis, also known as Odanak, became the destination of choice for those Maine natives seeking the support and security of the French. In 1705, Father Sebastian Rale established the Mission of St. Xavier at Becancour (Wowanak) below Quebec City. By the time of Queen Anne's War, Becancour would rival St. Francis as the home of the Kennebec and Penobscot people in exile.

Establishing residence within the mission villages of New France never provided an ideal solution to the problems facing the native people of Maine. While it provided immediate relief from the distress and danger of war, emigration represented displacement and separation from family ties, established social networks and traditional associations with ancestral homelands. Frequently, bands of native people sought refuge within one of the mission villages in the face of hunger and war, returning to their place of origin once the crisis

Abenaki of the French mission villages. *Courtesy of Wikimedia Commons.*

abated. However, some chose to establish semi-permanent residence at Becancour or St. Francis. Although they created new lives for themselves in French Canada, many exiles never relinquished the hope of reclaiming their lands in Maine from the English.

While life in the mission villages granted the residents safe haven and ready access to food, firearms and other trade goods, physical and material security came at a cost. Although the native people of the mission villages were able to come and go as they pleased and were able to maintain their own internal political structure, they remained fundamentally dependent on French aid and hospitality. Seeing the native people as ready allies in their war against the English, the French routinely used the flow of trade goods to exert influence over the native people's collective and individual choices of war and peace. When French requests for support did not align with native interests, the people of the mission villages exercised their own self-determination by dodging French appeals or using the porous nature of the communities to slip away on extended hunting excursions or otherwise temporarily remove themselves. Conversely, eruptions of violence with the English prompted the movement of people into the mission villages not only as sanctuary but also as bases of operation where the more militant factions of Maine's native people could obtain French aid and support. As the frontier wars progressed over the first half of the eighteenth century, native war parties striking the communities of coastal Maine increasingly originated from French Canada rather than from the resident native population.

By the outbreak of Queen Anne's War in 1703, a distinctive type of warfare had evolved in Maine and the Northeast in general. English, French and native people all participated in and contributed to the savage milieu of war that developed and tore Maine asunder during the seventeenth and eighteenth centuries. Civilian populations became not only legitimate but primary targets for military endeavors as the distinction between combatants and noncombatants was erased in the midst of unrestrained war.

Among the native people of Maine, war had a long and well-established tradition prior to the arrival of Europeans. Although the magnitude and technology of war changed dramatically for the native people of Maine following European contact, many traditional, ritualized customs were retained and adapted to the new environment of conflict that emerged during the seventeenth and eighteenth centuries. The rituals and customs that modern historians and anthropologists refer to as "mourning war" are important in understanding the nature of war as it developed on the Maine coast.[34] Among native people, war was viewed as an appropriate means to address real or perceived transgressions, including but not limited to murder, theft or significant affronts to a group's honor that could not be assuaged through ceremonial gift giving and exchange. While the destruction of one's enemies and the taking of scalps figured into the calculus of native war aims, the seizure of captives was the primary goal and most exalted achievement in the conduct of war.[35]

Warriors returning to their villages with enemy captives allowed the entire community to satiate their desire for justice or participate in an act of retribution. The fate of the captive lay in the hands of the community, which in many cases was guided by the desires of the group's matriarchs. Typically, the most valued captives were women and children, who were often absorbed into the tribe as laborers or in some cases as surrogates for lost family members. While young girls and women usually received the most preferential treatment, boys and young men were often subjected to grueling labor and indifferent treatment that bordered on neglect and cruelty. While some older boys and men were ritualistically killed, many more were used as collateral during negotiations or as hostage emissaries.

By the eighteenth century, the French in Canada had become active participants in the native tradition of mourning war. Native war parties returning to St. Francis and Becancour from raids along the Maine coast found willing buyers for captives who were not retained by the native people themselves. Rather than just meeting the social and symbolic needs inherent in the ritualized form of mourning war, captives became commodities to be traded between the natives and the French. Most captives sold to the French were employed as servants and laborers by wealthy French merchants and landholders,[36] while others were held in the hopes that they could be exchanged for Frenchmen in English custody. Aware of their captives' value, native warriors frequently went to great pains to see that their captives were delivered safely to Canada, and acts of wonton violence toward their prizes were uncommon. Although some captives perished as a result of illness or maltreatment during the course of their captivity, most English captives were eventually repatriated through ransom or prisoner exchange in accordance with the terms of peace negotiated at the end of each conflict. Some captives, particularly those who were taken as young children, refused to return to their English families and spent the remainder of their lives with the kinship group that absorbed them as one of their own.

The English adopted their own distinctively North American brand of warfare. Like their adversaries, the English would come to see men, women and children as lawful and justifiable targets of war and reprisal. Attacks against native domiciles became commonplace, and the taking of scalps and captives became regular practices in the English repertoire of war. During the seventeenth century, many captives taken by the English were sold into slavery, many going to near certain death on the sugar plantations of the West Indies. By the eighteenth century, captives were more typically held as diplomatic pawns and hostages. Public displays of vanquished foes became staples of the war culture in New England with the promotion of scalp taking. The scalps of native men, women and children became macabre commodities of war on the Maine frontier as public authorities authorized the payment of large cash rewards for the gruesome trophies.

In Maine, the English practice of offering cash inducements for the public display of slain enemies seems to have begun with the five-pound bounty offered by the residents of Monhegan for native heads in 1676. By the time of King William's War, the government of Massachusetts was offering substantial cash bounties for native scalps as incentive for men to offer their services as provincial soldiers or paramilitary volunteers. In September 1694, the General Court of Massachusetts officially sanctioned the practice of scalp- and captive-taking when it passed "An Act for Encouraging the Prosecution of the Indian Enemy and Rebels."[37] Section four of the act proclaimed, "For the encouragement to such as shall voluntarily go forth, in greater or lesser parties in the discovery and pursuit of the common enemy, that they be paid out of the public treasury, for every Indian, great or small, which they shall kill or take and bring in prisoner the sum of fifty pounds per head."[38]

From 1694 forward, Massachusetts regularly employed the use of scalp and captive bounties as tools in the prosecution of war against the people of the eastern tribes.

The peace following King William's War on the Maine coast was short-lived. During the four-year interlude between the end of King William's War and the outbreak of Queen Anne's War in 1703, both the government of Massachusetts and the leaders of the eastern tribes diligently sought to maintain peace on the Maine frontier. Trade and gift giving provided the cornerstones of peace in the wake of King William's War. In accordance with the terms negotiated at Mere Point, Massachusetts reopened trade with the eastern tribes, establishing permanent trading posts at Winter Harbor and the recently constructed fort at New Casco in Falmouth. In addition to the two permanent trading posts, Massachusetts outfitted a government-sponsored ship with the purpose of carrying trade to the native people of the midcoast and Penobscot Bay who were too far removed from the fort at New Casco to engage in convenient trade at that post. For the native people of Maine, the resumption of trade with the English and the increased efforts of Massachusetts to promote and regulate that trade filled a void created by the curtailment of trade with the French following King William's War. Financially weakened by a long, costly war and no longer requiring the military assistance of their native allies, the French dramatically reduced the material subsidies to which the people of the eastern tribes had become accustomed. By 1700, the value of French material aid earmarked for the native inhabitants of North America was reduced to only 10 percent of its wartime level.[39] Although the native residents of the mission villages in Canada still received some French aid, those people who remained in their homelands were increasingly forced to look toward their former enemies for material support.

Rumors of renewed war began to circulate soon after the outbreak of the War of Spanish Succession in Europe and England's declaration of war against France in 1702. Despite sporadic incidents of violence by both native people and whites along the midcoast, peace was maintained through diplomacy and ritual gift giving. Upon his arrival as the newly appointed royal governor of Massachusetts in 1702, Joseph Dudley made a priority of preserving the peace in Maine. On June 20, 1703, Dudley assembled the sagamores and principal leaders of the eastern tribes for a parley on the shores of Casco Bay to reaffirm the Mere Point Treaty and promote continued goodwill between Massachusetts and the native people of Maine. In resplendent dress, some 250 native attendees representing all the eastern tribes exchanged proclamations of harmony with their counterparts from Massachusetts.[40] The apparent success of the conference seemed to ensure continued peace in Maine for the foreseeable future.

The opportunity for peace proved to be elusive. Only fifty-one days after the peace conference at Casco Bay, war in all its fury returned. On August 10, 1703, a mixed force of French, pro-French Mohawks and native warriors from the Canadian mission villages descended on the communities of southern Maine in a series of coordinated attacks. Judge Samuel Penhallow, a contemporary observer, wrote, "The whole Eastern Country was in a Conflagration, no house standing, nor Garrison unattackt. August 10th at nine in the Morning they began their bloody Tragedy...and made a descent on the several Inhabitants from Casco to Wells at one and the same time, sparing none of every Age or Sex."[41]

As a result of the attacks, more than 250 inhabitants of Maine were killed, and another 150 were taken captive in the course of a single day. While the animus for the attack was rooted in the state of hostility between England and France, Governor Vaudreuil of Canada hoped the participation of Canadian Indians from the mission villages would undermine the peace in Maine and push the neutralist factions among the eastern tribes into conflict with their white neighbors. Despite desperate attempts to quell the violence in the wake of the attacks, the entire region was soon engulfed in what has become known as Queen Anne's War.

Throughout the war, the towns of southern Maine, coastal New Hampshire and the frontier towns of Massachusetts endured repeated onslaughts by French and Indian war parties. In Maine, multiple attacks were carried out against the towns of York, Kittery, Wells, Biddeford Pool (Saco), Winter Harbor (Saco) and Berwick. In response, Massachusetts regularly organized defensive patrols and long-range offensive scouts to impede and destroy the native people of Maine. Along the midcoast, periodic military excursions by Massachusetts brought Queen Anne's War to the doorstep of the Kennebec and Penobscot people. In a letter to his superiors in England, Governor Dudley indicated that during the autumn and winter of 1703 and 1704, he had 600 men in four parties who ranged as far as the Penobscot. In June 1704, Benjamin Church, at the head of 550 men supported by fourteen transports, thirty-six whaleboats and three warships,[42] reprised his

Benjamin Church. Church achieved notoriety as an Indian fighter during King Philip's War. During King William's War and Queen Anne's War, Church conducted several raids and expeditions against the native people of Maine and Acadia. *Collections of the Maine Historical Society.*

exploits of King William's War by ravaging the Maine coast from Penobscot Bay into the Bay of Fundy and down the western shore of Nova Scotia. At the head of Penobscot Bay, Church set upon several French and Penobscot families residing in the area, whereby he and his men "killed and took a considerable number of French and Indians."[43] As Church moved eastward, he devastated the coastal settlements of Acadia while disrupting the seasonal subsistence activities of the Penobscot, St. John and Cape Sable Indians. Although presented with the opportunity of assailing the Acadian capital of Port Royal, Church, with the council of his senior officers, decided against attacking the town and returned to the business of raiding the Maine coast. When Church returned to Boston after three months of campaigning, he was hailed as a hero and congratulated for his exploits by Governor Dudley before the General Court of Massachusetts.

The following winter, Massachusetts launched another military expedition, this time with the goal of bringing the Kennebec people to their knees. In February 1703/04, Lieutenant Colonel Winthrop Hilton, who had previously served as an officer under Benjamin Church, set off on snow shoes with 275 men, including 20 allied Indians, for the principal village of the Kennebec at Norridgewock. With twenty days of provisions carried on sleds pulled behind the men, Hilton's force proceeded through several feet of snow up the Kennebec River. Upon reaching Norridgewock, Hilton and his men discovered that the village, consisting of wigwams built around a

Catholic chapel and vestry, had been abandoned. Before retiring down the Kennebec, Hilton set fire to the village, leaving it to burn amid the snow and pines of the winter Maine woods.[44]

Throughout the remainder of the war, Massachusetts continued to send expeditions and scouts against the native people residing in the areas of the "old settlements," from the eastern reaches of Casco Bay to Pemaquid and Penobscot Bay. Most of these expeditions were seaborne operations, as in the case of Church's expedition of 1704 and the smaller expedition led by Colonel Walton in 1710–11, which consisted of 180 men aboard three sloops outfitted for war.[45] Although these expeditions rarely encountered the people whom they deemed the enemy, they effectively disrupted and destabilized their lives. A statement by Governor Dudley succinctly describes the effects of such operations against the eastern tribes: "This whole War I have kept them [the Indians] from all their Ancient Seats and planting grounds, and driven them to Inaccessible places and parts, where no Corn will grow for their support."[46]

As Governor Dudley described, the military activities of Massachusetts rendered the native people's situation untenable, and many fled initially to the mission village at St. Francis and, after 1705, to Becancour. Exile did not alleviate their suffering. In 1705, the French supply ship carrying aid for the people of the mission villages failed to arrive, and measles, to which they had no natural immunity, spread quickly among the crowded, hungry refugees. By 1706, those native people still residing in Maine began making remonstrances for peace and releasing English captives in their possession. Fearing that the native people of Maine were wavering in their commitment to the war, Governor Vaudreuil dispatched two Jesuit missionaries and a contingent of mission village Indians to reinvigorate their martial spirits and keep them engaged in the struggle against the English. In July 1710, the fervent desire for peace and trade compelled the Piqwacket, Penobscot and Kennebec people to send delegates to the fort at New Casco to beg for reconciliation with Massachusetts. Conferring with Captain Moody, the garrison's commander, the native representatives repeatedly denounced the French and requested supplies, stating that "otherwise they could not live and must return to y$^e$ French."[47] Unwilling to negotiate an accord and suspecting the native people of acting in a duplicitous manner, Massachusetts rejected the eastern tribes' petition. Failing in this bid for peace, war with all its miseries continued on the Maine coast for the next three years.

After more than ten years of war, peace between England and France was ratified in March 1713 with the Treaty of Utrecht. Significantly for the people of Maine, the twelfth article of the treaty ceded all of French

Acadia to the English, quelling the long-standing contention over French territorial limits in the region. This concession was brought about by the seizure of Port Royal in 1710 through a combined effort of New Englanders and the Royal Navy. The treaty allowed France to retain Isle Royal or Cape Breton Island at the northern end of Nova Scotia, where they established the fortified town of Louisbourg. News of peace and the Treaty of Utrecht reached North America three months later, leading to the conclusion of hostilities between Massachusetts and the eastern tribes with the signing of the Treaty of Portsmouth on July 11, 1713.

Like the Mere Point Treaty that ended King William's War, the Treaty of Portsmouth was a decidedly lopsided agreement. The treaty placed blame for the war on the native people, asserting that they had violated all other previous agreements. In consequence, the people of the eastern tribes were obliged to swear obedience to the Crown of Great Britain and disavow their ties to the French. Additionally, they agreed to allow English reoccupation of former settlements and to address any future grievances through the English legal system rather than through "private revenge."[48] As with the Mere Point Treaty, the only concession granted by Massachusetts was in regard to the resumption of regulated trade with Maine's native people.

The treaty was signed by eight sagamores of the Kennebec, Penobscot and St. John people. Although the native delegation lacked representatives from the Amarascoggin and the Piqwacket, the eight native signatories claimed authority to represent them as well. Following the ratification of the Treaty of Portsmouth, delegates from Massachusetts traveled to Casco Bay, where they called together additional representatives of the eastern tribes in an effort to ensure that the articles of the agreement were agreed to and understood by all of Maine's indigenous people. With further assurances of peace, the people of Maine prayed for a future of prosperity and peaceful coexistence with one another.

Queen Anne's War was a long and costly conflict for all the people of Maine. After ten years of war, it has been estimated that the white population declined by as much as 25 percent as a result of wartime losses and emigration.[49] Likewise, perhaps one-third of the region's native population disappeared from the rivers and forests of Maine as a result of the war.[50] With the onset of peace, many of Maine's native people returned from St. Francis and Becancour to reestablish lives in their traditional homelands. Within several years, new English settlers would begin pouring into midcoast Maine, setting the stage for renewed conflict.

Chapter 4

# Bringing It Home

Peace and people returned to Maine in the aftermath of Queen Anne's War. Although a proportion of Maine's expatriate native people opted to remain in Canada as residents of St. Francis and Becancour, many others returned to their homelands, where they hoped to reestablish their lives. On the Kennebec, Jesuit missionary Sebastian Rale and many of his former native parishioners returned to Norridgewock, where they rebuilt their destroyed mission village. Farther east, Father Lauverjat provided spiritual and political counsel to the people of the Penobscot nation who were also recovering from the effects of bitter and protracted war. Aware that the English would, by rights of the Treaty of Portsmouth, reoccupy their former settlements, the native people were entirely unprepared for the influx of white settlers seeking to call Maine home. Along the midcoast, where former English settlements had lain abandoned since the onset of King William's War more than twenty-five years before, renewed entrepreneurial efforts by the proprietors of the Pejeepscot and Muscongus Patents, the heirs of the Clarke and Lake Company and several smaller deed claimants fueled a new wave of white settlement.

The Pejeepscot Proprietors inaugurated the resettlement of Brunswick and Topsham with the construction of Fort George in 1715. The new fort was built near the former location of Fort Andros aside the lower falls of the Androscoggin River. Fort George was established not only with the intent to provide security and shelter for the nascent community planted around it but also with the express purpose of impeding the fisheries and principal canoe route for the area's native people.[51] The fort was constructed of stone measuring fifty feet on each side with bastions on each of the four corners. Located inside the fort was a two-story wooden building that served as the barracks for the fifteen men who garrisoned the fort under the command of Captain John Gyles.[52] At present Small Point in Phippsburg, the Pejeepscot Proprietors built a similar fort to protect the settlement of Augusta. Like Fort George, the fort at Augusta was built of stone encompassing a square of fifty feet on each side. On the fort's east and west corners were flankers likewise constructed of stone. Although well protected, the settlement at Augusta failed to flourish, and the General Court of Massachusetts rejected its application for incorporation in 1718. Farther up the Kennebec, on the western shore of Merrymeeting Bay, additional settlers under the Pejeepscot Patent established themselves in what is today Topsham and Bowdoinham. Widely distributed like a ribbon along the shoreline, the heart of this settlement was known as Somerset and located between the Cathance and Abagadaset Rivers. In 1720, Massachusetts provided for the defense of those settlers in the area of Somerset with a detachment of twenty soldiers posted on Swan Island. The following year, the Pejeepscot Proprietors began construction of a new outpost, Fort Richmond, on the west side of the river just above Swan Island.[53]

Along the eastern shore of the Kennebec River and Merrymeeting Bay, the heirs of the Clarke and Lake Company and Robert Temple began the resettlement of what is today Georgetown, Arrowsic, Woolwich and portions of Dresden. Whereas the original settlement under Clarke and Lake had been located in the northeast portion of Arrowsic, the community that emerged after 1714 was located on the southwest end of the island where the short-lived settlement of New Town had stood in the 1680s. The nucleus of the new community was a brick fort mounting several cannons and garrisoned initially by twenty soldiers provided by the Massachusetts Bay Colony.[54] Mills and houses were soon erected in the neighborhood of the fort, and by 1722, the village contained approximately thirty houses and other public buildings.[55] Farther up the Kennebec, nearly across Merrymeeting Bay from Somerset, Robert Temple established the sprawling community of Cork. Beginning just above the chops in modern Woolwich, the community stretched northward to the Eastern River in Dresden.

To the east, the agents of the Muscongus Patent worked energetically to establish a new community along the banks of the St. George River. In 1629, the Council of Plymouth awarded the Muscongus or Lincolnshire Patent to Thomas Leverett of Boston and John Beauchamp of London,

England. Upon Beauchamp's death in 1655, the entire patent passed on to Thomas Leverett. Little had been done with the patent during the seventeenth century with the exception of establishing a trading post in what is now Thomaston and a fishing station directly on the coast. In 1719, the patent was in the hands of John Leverett, the president of Harvard College and the grandson of Governor John Leverett. Not possessing the funds to adequately underwrite the development of the Muscongus Patent on his own, Leverett divided his holding into ten shares. One of the ten shares was awarded to Spencer Phips, the adopted son of and heir to Governor Sir William Phips. Aside from ready capital, Spencer Phips brought with him the deed to the area around Thomaston, Warren and Cushing that Sir William Phips had obtained from Madockawando at the time of the failed 1693 peace treaty at Pemaquid. Following the initial division of the patent, the company was further split into twenty additional shares, of which three were parceled out to Jonathan Waldo, Cornelius Waldo and Captain Thomas Westbrook. With financial backing secured, the proprietors of the Muscongus Patent erected a double sawmill, a fort with a garrison of twenty men and frames for houses in what is presently Thomaston.[56] They named their fledgling community Lincoln.

The creation of Lincoln caused immediate consternation among the local Penobscot people. While they and the other native people of Maine had agreed to let the English reestablish their former settlements at the conclusion of both King William's and Queen Anne's Wars, the Penobscot did not recognize the solitary seventeenth-century trading post on the banks of the St. George River as a genuine settlement and believed the new community violated their previous agreements with the English. Disagreement concerning the legitimacy of the Muscongus Patent's claim to the land on which Lincoln was sited compounded the controversy surrounding the new community. When the Penobscot pressed the proprietors of the Muscongus Patent about the origin of their deed, the proprietors indicated that Madockawando had sold the land to Sir William Phips, who, through his adopted son Spencer Phips, had effectively transferred the deed to the Muscongus Company. In response, the Penobscot asserted that Madockawando never possessed the authority to convey the land to Sir William Phips. In fact, the land deal in question had provoked outrage among the region's native people when it was brokered and was one of the primary reasons for the rejection of the 1693 Pemaquid peace treaty. In an effort to further distance themselves from Madockawando and his dealing with Phips, the Penobscot went on to claim enigmatically that Madockawando was not one of them, implying they were not bound by his agreement with Phips.[57] Unwilling to yield to the complaints of the local native population, agents of the Muscongus Patent continued their entrepreneurial enterprise, and Lincoln continued to be a source of contention between midcoast Maine's white and native people.

Just as Lincoln raised the ire of the Penobscot, the activities of the Pejeepscot Proprietors and Robert Temple along Merrymeeting Bay provoked the resentment of the Kennebec people. Over the winter of 1719–20, delegates from Massachusetts met with twenty-five representatives of the Kennebec people to discuss building tensions on the Maine frontier. During the course of the conference, the Kennebec party expressed dissatisfaction with the new settlements of Cork, Somerset and Swan Island on Merrymeeting Bay. As in the case of Lincoln, the Kennebec contested the validity of the deeds upon which English ownership of the land was based. According to the native delegates, the English had not obtained their deeds from the Kennebec but from the Amarascoggin, who did not possess authority to execute the deeds. Additionally, the native representatives indicated that aside from several trading posts, no English settlements had formerly been established as far up the Kennebec River as Cork, Swan Island and Somerset and that the new communities violated the terms of peace established at the end of King William's and Queen Anne's Wars. The native commissioners also complained of illicit and predatory trade, particularly in rum, by English residents along the river as another source of contention between the white and native populations.

Indeed, trade issues were undermining prospects for peaceful coexistence on the Maine frontier. Following both King William's and Queen Anne's Wars, Massachusetts agreed to regulate trade on the Maine frontier in an effort to prevent abuses by unscrupulous traders. By an act of the Massachusetts General Court in 1699, all trade with the region's native people was to be conducted by licensed traders at government-sanctioned and sponsored truck houses. Prices for the goods exchanged at the truck houses were established by the government and were to be posted and adhered to by the truck masters, who were responsible for overseeing the operation of the truck house. Through this system, native people were, in theory, ensured ready access to the material goods on which they had become dependent at reasonable and often heavily subsidized prices. The one item native people could not obtain through the truck house was alcohol. Because of alcohol's detrimental impact on native society and relations between natives and whites on the frontier,

# July 14th. 1703.
# Prices of Goods

### Supplyed to the
## Eastern Indians,

By the feveral Truckmasters ; and of the Peltry received by the Truckmasters of the faid *Indians.*

ONe yard Broad Cloth, *three* Beaver skins, *in feafon.*
One yard & half Gingerline, *one* Beaver skin, *in feafon*
One yard Red or Blew Kerfey, *two* Beaver skins, *in feafon.*
One yard good Duffels, *one* Beaver skin, *in feafon.*
One yard & half broad fine Cotton, *one* Beaver skin, *in feafon*
*Two* yards of Cotton, *one* Beaver skin, *in feafon.*
One yard & half of half thicks, *one* Beaver skin, *in feafon.*
*Five* Pecks Indian Corn, *one* Beaver skin, *in feafon.*
*Five* Pecks Indian Meal, *one* Beaver Skin. *in feafon.*
*Four* Pecks Peafe, *one* Beaver skin, *in feafon.*
*Two* Pints of Powder, *one* Beaver skin, *in feafon.*
One Pint of Shot, *one* Beaver skin, *in feafon.*
*Six* Fathom of Tobacco, *one* Beaver skin, *in feafon.*
*Forty* Biskets, *one* Beaver skin, *in feafon.*
*Ten* Pound of Pork, *one* Beaver skin, *in feafon.*
*Six* Knives, *one* Beaver skin, *in feafon.*
*Six* Combes, *one* Beaver skin, *in feafon.*
*Twenty* Scaines Thread, *one* Beaver skin, *in feafon.*
One Hat, *two* Beaver skins, *in feafon.*
One Hat with Hatband, *three* Beaver skins, *in feafon.*
*Two* Pound of large Kettles, *one* Beaver skin, *in feafon.*
*One* Pound & half of fmall Kettles, *one* Beaver skin, *in feafon*
One Shirt, *one* Beaver skin, *in feafon.*
One Shirt with Ruffels, *two* Beaver skins, *in feafon.*
*Two* Small Axes, *one* Beaver skin, *in feafon.*
*Two* Small Hoes, *one* Beaver skin, *in feafon.*
*Three* Dozen middling Hooks, *one* Beaver skin, *in feafon.*
One Sword Blade, *one* & *half* Beaver skin, *in feafon.*

*What fhall be accounted in Value equal*
*One* Beaver *in* feafon : *Viz.*

ONe Otter skin in feafon, is *one* Beaver

One Bear skin in feafon, is *one* Beaver,

*Two* Half skins in feafon, is *one* Beaver

*Four* Pappcote skins in feafon, is *one* Beaver

*Two* Foxes in feafon, is *one* Beaver.

*Two* Woodchocks in feafon, is *one* Beaver.

*Four* Martins in feafon, is *one* Beaver.

*Eight* Muncks in feafon, is *one* Beaver.

*Five* Pounds of Feathers, is *one* Beaver.

*Four* Raccoones in feafon, is *one* Beaver.

*Four* Seil skins large, is *one* Beaver.

*One* Moofe Hide, is *two* Beavers.

*One* Pound of Caflorum, is *one* Beaver.

Truck house price schedule. Government-sponsored trading posts known as truck houses were required to post the prices and rates of exchange for the various goods that flowed through them. This reproduction reflects the prices as of July 14, 1703. *Courtesy of Ken Hamilton.*

the sale of rum to native traders, either by individuals or through the truck houses, was prohibited by Massachusetts. Unable to procure rum legally, native people engaged in an unregulated, often predatory black market trade with complicit white neighbors to acquire the drug.

Following King William's War, Massachusetts established truck houses at the fort at New Casco (Falmouth) and Fort Mary (Saco). For the Penobscot and Kennebec people, these truck houses proved to be too far removed from their habitations for them to conduct regular and convenient trade. Massachusetts attempted to accommodate the eastern tribes and remedy the situation by providing a ship outfitted for trade to ply the waters of midcoast Maine, but this, too, failed to meet the native people's need for consistent access to European goods. By 1720, the people of the eastern tribes were expressing dissatisfaction not only with the inconveniences of trade associated with the location of current truck houses but also with the devaluation of their primary trade commodity, beaver skins. During the first quarter of the eighteenth century, European demand for beaver skins was beginning to abate due to changing fashion trends, precipitating a slide in the commodity's value. Not understanding the economic mechanisms behind the value for their skins, the native people felt beguiled and abused as the value of their exchanges diminished relative to the price of the goods they sought to obtain from the English.

Amid growing tension over land and trade issues, sporadic incidents of violence occasioned fears of renewed hostilities in Maine. Through ongoing discourse and negotiation, Massachusetts and the eastern tribes sought to maintain peace in the region. In late November 1720, commissioners from Massachusetts met with the principal leaders of the Norridgewock at Arrowsic to seek redress for recent confrontations in which cattle were killed and white settlers threatened. As compensation for the recent spate of property damage, Massachusetts demanded the payment of two hundred beaver skins and the surrender of four native people as collateral hostages to assure payment of the skins and continued peaceful relations. When the Norridgewock pressed the Massachusetts delegation about removing the settlements on Merrymeeting Bay, the tone of the negotiations quickly soured, provoking the following response by Massachusetts:

> *The Claims of the English to these Lands in the Kennebec river have been Examined, & we are fully satisfied yt the English have a good title thereunto as appears by their Deeds & Converances from the Indians, Above 70 years since; An ye Governm[t] resolved to defend the Proprietors in these their Just Rights. It is therefore in vain for you to Expect yt ever those Inhabitants will be removed—The Government is very loth to draw the sword which you have given them just provocation to do. But you may depend upon it that the forces which have been raised at a vast Expense for y[e] curbing your Insolence, will not be disbanded till you have complied with the Obligation, you have now laid your selves under And if you will constrain us with your*

*repeat'd Insults to any Violent proceedings, we have force enough: & will*
*pursue you to your Headquarters & will not leave you till we have cut you*
*off Root and Branch from ye Face of the Earth.*[58]

Having been threatened and humiliated, the Norridgewock representatives resentfully agreed to comply with the demands of Massachusetts. Rather than promoting the continuation of peace in the region, the proceedings at Arrowsic only fanned the flames of discord already engulfing coastal Maine.

Tension and frustration continued to foment in Maine during the months following the conference at Arrowsic. In August 1721, a flotilla of ninety canoes bearing an estimated two hundred Indians returned to Arrowsic. The native party appeared before Captain John Penhallow well armed, well dressed and flying French flags to present him with a letter addressed to Massachusetts governor Samuel Shute. In attendance with the native party were Father Sebastian Rale and two other Frenchmen, one a Jesuit missionary and the other a French military officer, both of whom had been sent to the Maine frontier on the orders of Canadian governor Vaudreuil as envoys to the more militant factions of the Norridgewock. The appearance of a native delegation flying French colors accompanied by Father Rale, Father de la Chase and Lieutenant de Croisel served to confirm long-held suspicions by Massachusetts of French influence undermining the fragile peace in Maine. The letter that Captain Penhallow forwarded to Governor Shute appeared to be drafted with the consent of all the eastern tribes and declared, "If the settlers did not remove in three weeks, the Indians would come and kill them all, destroy their cattle and burn their houses"[59] and that "you Englishmen have taken away the lands which the Great God has given our fathers and us."[60]

In response to the letter, Massachusetts declared the eastern tribes to be in a state of rebellion and authorized three hundred men to be raised as soldiers for service in Maine. Furthermore, Massachusetts called upon the eastern tribes to surrender all Jesuit missionaries and rebels in their midst. When the Norridgewock failed to surrender Father Rale, Massachusetts attempted to seize him by force. In December 1721, a detachment of provincial soldiers led by Captain Thomas Westbrook ascended the Kennebec River to seize Father Rale at the Norridgewock mission village. The approach of Westbrook and his men had been observed, enabling Rale to evade his would-be captors and disappear into the Maine woods. Although Westbrook and his men returned without their query, they did manage to secure Father Rale's strongbox containing his correspondence with Governor Vaudreuil. The content of the

Sebastian Rale's strongbox. Massachusetts authorities believed that Jesuit missionary Sebastian Rale had been inciting the Norridgewock Indians on behalf of the French. Rale's strongbox was obtained by Massachusetts during an attempt to seize him and bring him to trial for his seditious activities. Correspondence found in the box between Rale and the governor of New France, Vaudreuil, confirmed Massachusetts's suspicions. *Collections of the Maine Historical Society.*

letters served as confirmation that the French, through their agents in Maine, were working to agitate and inflame the resentment of the native people toward their English neighbors and the government of Massachusetts.

Despite several attempts to resolve tensions and restore peace over the winter, Maine was again plunged into bitter war during the spring of 1722. On June 13, a party of approximately sixty native warriors seized nine families residing around Merrymeeting Bay. All but five of the captives were released within days of being taken. Those who were not released were kept as counter collateral for the four Norridgewock hostages surrendered to Massachusetts the previous year. Over the next several days, sporadic attacks occurred across the midcoast. At Damariscove Island, a fishing vessel was attacked, as were isolated homesteads in Damariscotta, Pemaquid and

Broad Cove on Muscongus Bay. The largest attack in the opening salvo of war was directed against the new and easternmost English community of Lincoln (Thomaston). On June 15, two hundred native warriors fell upon St. George's fort and laid waste to the new community, burning the mills, homes and a sloop laden with supplies in the river. After taking five captives and killing cattle, the war party retired and disappeared.

Further attacks occurred across the region during the summer of 1722. In July, Fort George in Brunswick was attacked while the community was burned. The settlements of Cork and Somerset were reduced to ashes at this time as well. In late August, St. George's fort was assailed again and subjected to a twelve-day siege. Unable to take the fort by direct assault, the besiegers attempted to undermine the fort's walls by digging beneath them. The native stratagem for taking the fort was foiled when heavy rains caused the collapse of the tunnel, burying the attackers alive. Failing to take the fort by storm or force the surrender of the garrison, the native attackers withdrew in early September, leaving behind twenty native and five English corpses.

Several days later, a large force of St. Francis and Cape Sable (Micmac) Indians descended on the community at Arrowsic. Most of the inhabitants withdrew to the safety of the fort and several other fortified garrison houses, while the native war party proceeded to kill cattle and burn the majority of the houses in the area. A relief party consisting of men from Colonel Walton's command in Casco Bay, the fort at Augusta (Small Point) and Merrymeeting Bay launched a counterattack against the native attackers but was beaten back by superior numbers. Having destroyed the settlement at Arrowsic and unwilling to conduct a protracted siege of the fort, the war party retreated up the Kennebec River under the cover of darkness, briefly harassing Fort Richmond on its way back north.

Having declared war against the eastern tribes in response to the summer's wave of attacks, Massachusetts began raising an army with the intent of carrying the war home to Maine's native people. To encourage participation in the war effort, Massachusetts, as had become customary, authorized the establishment of scalp and captive bounties. For each adult scalp, volunteers receiving neither pay nor provisions from the government were promised £100.[61] Those receiving rations and those receiving pay and rations were offered £60 and £15, respectively. A total of one thousand men were authorized for service on the eastern frontier, with three hundred men earmarked for an expedition against the Penobscot and four hundred men to range the coast in defensive patrols. The remaining three hundred men were

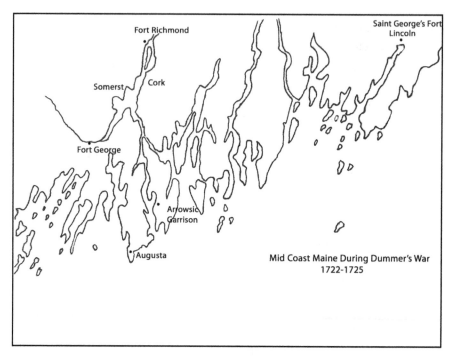

*Author's map.*

allocated to garrisons from the Piscataqua to the Kennebec Rivers,[62] with another twenty-five to be posted at St. George.[63] Overall command of the forces on the eastern frontier was given to Colonel Shadrack Walton, who had served in Maine during Queen Anne's War, commanding the 1710–11 raids along the downeast coast. Walton never raised the full complement of men authorized by Massachusetts, and the proposed expedition against the Penobscot failed to materialize. With dissatisfaction mounting against Walton during the autumn of 1722, he was replaced as the senior commander on the Maine frontier by Thomas Westbrook.

Upon assuming command, Westbrook reinvigorated efforts to launch an offensive against the Penobscot. On February 11, 1722/23, Westbrook set sail from the Kennebec with 230 men to range the Maine coast as far east as Mount Desert Island. After cruising the immediate shore, Westbrook proceeded to search for the main village of the Penobscot people. On March 4, Westbrook and his flotilla came to anchor near the mouth of the Penobscot River, whereupon he dispatched a party to seek out the Penobscot community. After five days of marching through the woods, the reconnaissance party spotted the palisaded village approximately thirty-two miles upriver. Leaving one hundred men to guard his supplies, Westbrook marched with the main body of his army to attack the village. Shortly after six o'clock on the evening of March 9, Westbrook's men fell upon the village only to find it deserted. In a subsequent letter to Lieutenant Governor Dummer, Westbrook described the village: "The Fort was 70 yards in Length and 50 in breadth. Well stockado'd 14 foot high furnisht with 23 houses Built reguler; On the South Side close by it was their Chappell, 60 foot Long and 30 wide Well and handsomely finish'd within and without and on $y^e$ South of that $y^e$ Fryers Dwelling house."[64]

After setting fire to the village, Westbrook and his men returned to their transports at the mouth of the river. On March 20, the expedition returned to the fort and charred community at St. George.

At the same time Westbrook was proceeding against the Penobscot, Captain Johnson Harmon was leading an expedition on snowshoes through the Maine woods against the Kennebec village at Norridgewock. In an effort to avoid detection, Harmon chose a circuitous route up the Androscoggin River, from whence he planned to cross overland to the Sandy River, which emptied into the Kennebec near the site of the mission village. Encountering poor ice conditions due to a stretch of mild and rainy weather, Harmon was forced to abandon the planned attack before reaching his intended target. Mother Nature, at least temporarily, saved Norridgewock from the wrath of the English.

The spring of 1723 bore witness to renewed native attacks against the communities of southern Maine. Falmouth (Portland, South Portland, Westbrook and Cape Elizabeth), Berwick, Wells, York, Scarborough and Saco were all assailed. The midcoast provided few targets for native war parties by 1723. The few people who remained from Brunswick eastward to St. George resided in fortified garrisons and conducted the routines of their daily lives under the watchful eye of armed guards, never far from the protective palisades and reinforced walls of the garrisons. Loath to expose themselves before well-defended forts and garrisons, lurking native war parties chose instead to target exposed, isolated and unprepared targets of opportunity.

Believing they had found such a target, a war party of approximately sixty warriors descended upon St. George's fort on Christmas Day 1723. Over the past several months, the fort's garrison had been reduced as a result of disease and, more importantly, Massachusetts's waning commitment to bankrolling the outpost. During the fall, the future of St. George's fort had been the topic of an ongoing debate in the General Court of Massachusetts. Although

The palisade fence and blockhouse built of squared wooden timbers exemplify the typical arrangement of the fortified garrisons and forts dotting the Maine coast throughout the period. *Author's photo.*

friction between the legislative and executive branches of government lay at the heart of the debate, the destruction of the Penobscot's village by Thomas Westbrook, the isolated nature of the post and a belief that the government was propping up the interests of the Muscongus Patent caused some within the General Court to question the necessity of maintaining the post at government expense. By mid-December, a compromise had been reached regarding the fort's disposition. Although the fort would be maintained on the government establishment, the garrison would be reduced to a skeleton force of twelve men under the command of a sergeant.[65] Learning of the fort's weakened circumstances through recently obtained captives, native war leaders recognized an opportunity to strike a symbolic and strategically significant blow to the English by seizing their easternmost outpost, the loss of which would roll the frontier back at least as far as the Kennebec River. In a rare display of determination before a strongly fortified position, the native war party conducted a protracted siege of St. George's fort. Despite their situation, the garrison endured and persevered for thirty days. The siege was finally broken by the arrival of a relief force under the command of Thomas Westbrook. In the following months, the General Court revised its estimation of the post's importance, and the garrison was once again strengthened to bolster the eastern frontier.

Raids against the settlements of Maine resumed in March 1724 with attacks against Cape Pourpose, Scarborough, Kennebunk and Berwick. More than thirty people were killed, wounded or taken captive as a result of the attacks. As had happened during the previous year, native war parties routinely looked for targets of opportunity beyond the protection of the local forts and garrisons. In late April, Captain Josiah Winslow, the newly appointed commander of St. George's fort, led a party of sixteen men down the St. George River in two whaleboats, one under his command and the other under a Sergeant Harvey, with the design of disrupting the natives' procurement of waterfowl near the river's mouth. Not finding any signs of native hunters, Winslow and his men began the journey back up the river the following day. Along the way, the two boats became separated, and the men of Sergeant Harvey's whaleboat partook in their own duck hunting. When Harvey's whaleboat approached the shore to retrieve a duck shot by one of his men, the boat came under attack from natives hidden along the bank. Attempting to aid Sergeant Harvey and his men, Captain Winslow turned his boat around but was quickly surrounded by a swarm of canoes. Both sides exchanged musket shots, and the natives in their canoes closed on the whaleboats, attempting to effect a boarding. A hand-to-hand struggle ensued between the occupants of the canoes and the whaleboats. Eventually, Winslow, although seriously wounded, made it to shore, where he and the other survivors mounted a final but ineffectual last stand. Only three of Winslow's party survived, all of whom were Indians allied to the English. They were sent back to the fort with ominous news of the encounter.[66]

With targets of opportunity becoming increasingly difficult to find in the shadow of the garrisons and the watchful eye of provincial and volunteer soldiers, native war parties turned their attention to a new set of targets along coastal Maine. Setting their sights on the harbors and islands lying beyond the protective reach of the strong points and patrols, native assailants seized a total of twenty boats of varying sizes, including one schooner, over the course of the summer.[67] Although upward of twenty sailors were killed in the course of the attacks, the natives retained far more of the ships' crews as captives, particularly the ships' masters and experienced sailors, to help operate the vessels.[68] Hopping from harbor to harbor and island to island, this native band of pirates proceeded to acquire vessels and strike exposed targets on shore.

In July 1724, the native fleet sailed up the coast in yet another attempt to force the surrender of St. George's fort. In his report regarding the attack, Captain William Canady, the fort commander, stated that shortly after the fort's watch spotted the approach of five vessels coming up the St. George River, a group of natives appeared at the back of the fort with a flag of truce. After making repeated demands for the fort's surrender and being rebuffed by Captain Canady, the natives began their assault. The natives poured musket fire on the fort's walls and flankers while sending several of their captured ships, laden with combustibles and set ablaze, toward the fort's outworks along the river. It is unclear whether one of the fire ships made contact with its target or if native parties on land attempted to set fire to the fort's walls and palisades, for Canady states, "While the vessels were burning they kept firing on all sides but we held them in Play and by heaving on water we prevent the fires doing any damage."[69] After several hours of fighting and failing in their bid to engulf the fort in flames, the native war party ceased their attack and slipped down the river under the cover of darkness.

Concerned by the threat this native fleet posed, Massachusetts and New Hampshire organized a joint effort to combat the flotilla. Several vessels were outfitted—including three shallops with forty men and a larger schooner with a complement of twenty—to pursue the numerically superior native fleet off the Maine coast. Finding their query, the English engaged the native flotilla in a brief skirmish. During the fighting, the sails and rigging of the English schooner were sheared away by native cannon fire, necessitating the temporary abandonment of the English pursuit.[70] Seeking the protective shelter of the Penobscot River, the native flotilla deployed to repulse the inevitable English attempt at its destruction. As the English squadron made its approach up the river, it was raked by withering musket fire from native warriors on the shore and forced to retreat. Although the English failed to destroy the native pirate fleet, no further seaborne attacks were carried out against the English in 1724, and the hijacked vessels seem to have disappeared by the winter of 1725.

Having unsuccessfully attempted to destroy the principal village of the Kennebec people at Norridgewock already during the war, Massachusetts launched another foray into the heart of Maine in the summer of 1724. Hoping to catch the native population at their village during the time of their corn harvest, the expedition pushed off from Fort Richmond toward the end of August. In seventeen whaleboats, 208 men in four companies under the overall command of Captain Johnson Harmon threaded their way up the Kennebec River toward their intended target.[71] Aside from destroying the village, Captain Harmon was ordered to finally seize Father Sebastian Rale for his subversive activities among the Kennebec people. The approach of the Massachusetts force was nearly betrayed when it encountered the family of a well-known and respected Kennebec sagamore known as Bomazeen while portaging around the falls in present Skowhegan. Killing Bomazeen and his daughter, the force continued on undetected with Bomazeen's wife in tow as a captive.

The expedition arrived before the village at Norridgewock unnoticed on the afternoon of August 23. Observing the village from a distance, Harmon and his men noted wisps of smoke rising from the cornfields beyond the village. Hoping to apprehend people at work in the fields, Harmon with sixty men marched around the village toward the cornfields and the mouth of the Sandy River. Captain Jeremiah Moulton was given the task of taking the village. Moulton positioned two of his companies in ambush to prevent the people from escaping while he moved forward with his own company to assault the village. Moulton's attack came as a complete surprise. Unarmed as Moulton's force entered the village, the men of Norridgewock offered ineffective resistance as the women, children and elderly fled for their lives. With the river the only possible route of escape, panicked people attempted to swim to the opposite shore or scramble aboard canoes, many of which had no paddles. They were pursued by Moulton's men, who poured musket fire into the confused, huddled mass of people thronging the Kennebec. When the killing was done, Mouton and Harmon, who returned from the cornfield finding it devoid of people, set fire to the village.

It is impossible to provide a firm estimate on the number of Norridgewock who lost their lives in the assault. Perhaps as many as eighty men, women and children, young and old alike, perished that day, many of whom drowned, their bodies drifting down the Kennebec with the current.[72] Among the bodies that littered the village itself was that of Father Sebastian Rale. Moulton had specifically ordered his men to take Rale alive, but in the chaos of the onslaught, Rale was killed and scalped. The expedition returned to Fort Richmond on August 27 with twenty-eight scalps, three redeemed English captives and four native prisoners.[73] Of the twenty-eight scalps, only six belonged to adult males; the other twenty-two belonged to women or children. Harmon was lauded as a hero upon his return to Boston, and Samuel Penhallow of Arrowsic proclaimed the attack "the greatest victory we have obtained in the three or four last wars."[74] For the people of Norridgewock, the attack was an unmitigated disaster. In grief, the shattered remnants of their people removed themselves to the security of St. Francis and the French.

Repeated offensives by Massachusetts throughout the winter and spring of 1724–25 sowed further destruction among the region's native people. In western Maine, Captain John Lovewell of Dunstable, Massachusetts, commanding a company of volunteers, led three expeditions against the Piqwacket residing along the upper reaches of the Saco River. Lovewell's second raid in February 1724/25 was deemed a resounding success and netted more than £1,000 in scalp bounties for himself and his men.[75] Having established a formidable reputation as a scalp hunter, Lovewell had no difficulty organizing another expedition in April 1725. Setting off mid-month, the men under his command held high expectations of a profitable excursion and a hero's welcome upon their return. Their hopes proved illusory; they were ambushed and decimated in the course of a daylong firefight with a party of Piqwacket in what is presently Fryeburg on May 8. Although most of Lovewell's men lost their lives to the Piqwacket, the losses to the Piqwacket themselves are believed to have been substantial. Having suffered on several occasions at Lovewell's hands in the course of only several months and believing that Massachusetts would continue to organize offensives against their homelands, most of the Piqwacket people, like the Norridgewock, abandoned their homes in Maine, seeking refuge in Canada.

As the remnants of Lovewell's men were making their way home through the woods of southwestern Maine, another expedition was pushing off from Fort Richmond on Merrymeeting Bay. Ascending the Kennebec and Sebasticook Rivers, Captain Joseph Heath and his men intended to strike yet another blow against the Penobscot people. In the two years since Thomas Westbrook had destroyed their principal village, the Penobscot had reestablished a sizable community in what is today Bangor. Heath's approach was likely noticed. When he and his men arrived at the stockaded village, they found it unoccupied. As had become customary in war on the Maine frontier, Heath had the village burned before making his return via the coast to St. George's fort. Upon reaching St. George, Heath learned of recent appeals for peace by the Penobscot people.

By the spring of 1725, the situation had become unbearable for the native people of Maine. Three years of war had left them gaunt shadows of their former selves. Repeated forays into their homelands by soldiers and volunteers of the Massachusetts Bay Colony caused tremendous loss, hardship and disruption for the Penobscot and their Abenaki brethren to the west. Hungry, in need of European manufactured goods and desperate for physical security, many of Maine's native people flocked to the French mission villages of St. Francis and Becancour. Accepting the flood of refugees with open arms, the French offered considerable rhetorical support but no material aid for the native war effort. Exhausted and unable to continue prosecuting a losing war, the native people of Maine sought an end to hostilities during the summer of 1725.

Following a preliminary conference at St. George on July 2, 1725, the Penobscot, who had assumed diplomatic leadership for Maine's native people, agreed to send a peace delegation to Boston in November. Over the course of a month, the Penobscot, claiming to represent all the eastern tribes and the residents of the mission villages, met with Massachusetts peace commissioners and Lieutenant Governor William Dummer to negotiate an end to the hostilities in Maine. The resulting peace accord, which has come to be known as Dummer's Treaty, was signed on December 15, 1725. In addition to reaffirming the agreements ending King William's and Queen Anne's Wars, Dummer's Treaty, at least on paper, radically altered the relationship between Massachusetts and the Penobscot. Under the terms of the treaty, the Penobscot, and by extension all of Maine's native people, accepted "the Sovereignty of the Crown of Great Britain and their Subjection thereto."[76] Additionally, the Penobscot agreed "that in case any of the Tribes of Indians intended to be included in this Treaty shall

Notwithstanding continue or renew Acts of Hostility against the English or refuse to confirm this present Treaty entered into on their behalf, in such case the Penobscot Tribe to covenant and engage with us in reducing them to Reason."[77]

In acknowledging their subjection to the Crown of Great Britain and agreeing to support the English militarily in any further conflicts between the white and native populations of Maine, the Penobscot effectively surrendered their autonomy to Massachusetts and the King of England. It is unclear how the interpreters provided by Massachusetts presented the above-referenced treaty articles to the native signatories, as divergent understandings of the agreement would subsequently surface between Massachusetts and the Penobscot.

During the peace conference, contention arose between Massachusetts and the native envoys regarding the continued English occupation of Fort Richmond, St. George's fort and the surrounding settlements. Reiterating concerns regarding the propriety of the deeds on which the establishment of the communities and forts were based, the Penobscot delegation proffered that the abandonment of Merrymeeting Bay and the St. George River would greatly reduce tension in Maine and serve to prove Massachusetts's inclination toward peace. Certain of their deeds' validity, Massachusetts refused to relinquish either of the holdings. As a concession, Massachusetts agreed to establish truck houses at both Fort Richmond and St. George's fort to facilitate trade with the eastern tribes. Additionally, Massachusetts agreed to prohibit settlement beyond Fort Richmond on the Kennebec River and above the falls of the St. George River in what is today the village of Warren.

In August 1726, seeking to assure broad-based consensus among the native people for Dummer's Treaty, Massachusetts called for additional native representatives to ratify the understanding brokered the previous December. On August 6, commissioners from Massachusetts, New Hampshire and Nova Scotia conferred with approximately forty sagamores and principal leaders of the Penobscot and St. John people at Falmouth (Portland). Claiming to rightfully represent all the eastern people, including the people residing in St. Francis and Becancour, Wenemovet—the party's chief sagamore—and twenty-five other native leaders affixed their names to the treaty, officially restoring peace to Maine.[78]

In the wake of Dummer's War, the Penobscot assumed the mantle of diplomatic leadership among the vanquished native people of Maine. Although factional nuances existed within and between the kinship bands of the Penobscot people, those who chose to remain in Maine rather than remove themselves to the mission villages genuinely and faithfully sought reconciliation with their English neighbors. Seeing accommodation and diplomatic alignment with Massachusetts as the best means of preserving the peace they so desperately desired, the Penobscot of Maine occupied an uneasy middle ground between their more militant native brethren in Canada and the region's white population with whom they shared a bitter and acrimonious history.

Chapter 5

# Fear and Fatigue

The most protracted period of peace since 1675 settled over the Maine coast following Dummer's War. Renewed stability in the region prompted a new influx of European inhabitants who reestablished and expanded the communities of the midcoast. Arriving in America beginning in the early eighteenth century, waves of immigrants from Northern Ireland, known today as the Scots-Irish, established themselves on the frontiers of colonial America from Appalachia to Maine. From Casco Bay eastward, they constituted the majority of the region's population from 1715 onward. Cape Elizabeth, Falmouth, North Yarmouth (Yarmouth, Freeport, Harpswell), Brunswick, Topsham, Arrowsic, Cork and Somerset were all Scots-Irish enclaves. In the years following Dummer's War, the Scots-Irish would go on to inhabit the new and reclaimed settlements at Wiscasset, Townsend (Boothbay), Pemaquid, Bristol, Walpole, Harrington, Damariscotta, Newcastle and St. George.

Although sharing a common language and a similar Protestant religious background with the English inhabitants of New England, the first waves of Scots-Irish immigrants received a cold reception upon their arrival in Boston. Deemed unmannered, uneducated, unruly, uncivilized and undesirable by the Puritan establishment of Massachusetts, the Scots-Irish found themselves unwelcome amid the inveterate communities surrounding Boston. Initially, the Scots-Irish gravitated to the frontier of New Hampshire and the shores of Casco Bay. Within a few short years, many of the original immigrants, as well as subsequent new arrivals, made their way eastward to the lower Kennebec and Merrymeeting Bay. Coinciding with attempts by proprietary landholders to reestablish the abandoned communities of coastal Maine, the arrival of large numbers of Scots-Irish immigrants provided the proprietors with the human capital necessary to further their endeavors. Unable to attract settlers from the more stable communities of New England, the proprietors embraced the Scots-Irish who, hazarding the lives and security of their families, looked to create new opportunities for themselves in the uncertain, war-torn borderland of coastal Maine.

Historically, the Scots-Irish were people of the borderlands. Originating in the lowlands of Scotland and the northern fringes of England, they had endured centuries of poverty, warfare and fragmented sociopolitical organization before arriving in America. Pervasive violence, weak social institutions and ever-shifting boundaries created a tradition of locally vested authority based on kinship and clan relations. Conflict between rival and competing clans as well as repeated attempts by the English to subjugate the lowland Scots perpetually stunted economic prosperity in the region and produced generations of individuals who were self-reliant, suspicious of outsiders, resistant to external authority and accustomed to settling differences through violence.

During the seventeenth century, many lowland Scots were enticed to take part in the English colonization of Ulster in Northern Ireland. Looking to escape the poverty and uncertainty of life along the border of England and Scotland, many of the region's inhabitants responded to the allure of inexpensive leases offered by English landlords in Northern Ireland. Life in Ulster proved to be no more secure than life in the lowlands. For more than a century, the Protestant Scottish immigrants were embroiled in a series of conflicts rooted in the period's wars of religious faith and with a native Irish population unwilling to yield their ancestral homelands to invaders from across the North Sea. By the beginning of the eighteenth century, many Ulster Scots, who by this time considered themselves Irish, were pressured to leave Ireland for the shores of North America in the face of recurrent crop failures, economic distress, religious persecution and social disenfranchisement. These Scots-Irish immigrants brought with them a cultural heritage that shaped their relationships with their Native American neighbors, the provincial government of Massachusetts and the representatives of that government who lived in their midst. The Scots-Irish antipathy toward government policy developed in Boston, and their propensity for taking the law into their own hands would, over time, help unravel the fragile peace in Maine.

76

Initial efforts to reestablish settlements east of the Kennebec River in the wake of Dummer's War were rekindled through the enterprise of Colonel David Dunbar. In addition to holding a colonel's commission in the British army, Dunbar occupied the lucrative and influential offices of the surveyor of the king's woods and lieutenant governor of Nova Scotia.[79] In 1729, by the authority of King George II, he proclaimed the creation of a new Crown colony known as Sagadahoc. The territorial bounds of the new colony encompassed the formerly disputed lands of Acadia, ranging from the Kennebec to the St. Croix River. Incidentally, the inability of Massachusetts to adequately defend this territory during prior conflicts was cited as rationale for stripping the Bay Colony of its authority over this region. Dunbar's first act in reopening the lands of the midcoast was to rebuild the fort at Pemaquid, which he named Fort Frederick in honor of King George's son and heir apparent, the Prince of Wales. Of Scots-Irish descent himself, Dunbar sought to populate the newly created towns of Townsend (Boothbay), Walpole, Harrington and Damariscotta with other Scots-Irish settlers from the frontier communities of New Hampshire and Casco Bay. With promises of cheap land and easy title, more than 150 families took up residence between the Kennebec River and Muscongus Bay within a few years.[80]

Boston's political and financial elites raised immediate and vehement objections to Dunbar's creation of Sagadahoc. Incensed by the usurpation of Massachusetts's authority over the region, Governor Jonathan Belcher went so far as to threaten the use of military force to unseat Dunbar and retake the midcoast. Expressly warned against armed confrontation by the Crown, Massachusetts initiated legal proceedings with the Board of Trade, Britain's administrative apparatus responsible for overseeing colonial affairs, seeking redress for the loss of eastern Maine.

Unquestionably, the greatest potential losers in the brewing crisis were the stockholders of the Muscongus Patent, whose claim fell wholly within the bounds of Dunbar's new province of Sagadahoc. Supporting Massachusetts's appeal to the Board of Trade, the company dispatched Samuel Waldo, the son of Jonathan Waldo, a wealthy and influential Boston merchant and a shareholder of the Muscongus Patent, to London as their representative in the case. In 1731, through the efforts of Waldo and Massachusetts's agent in London, the Board of Trade reversed its support of Dunbar's claim and reestablished Massachusetts's authority over Maine as far east as the St. Croix River. Having helped secure clear title to its claim, the Muscongus Company awarded Waldo a controlling share of the company's stock in

Samuel Waldo was one of the leading figures in the development of midcoast Maine during the mid-eighteenth century. As a proprietor, merchant, legislator and soldier, Waldo is generally underappreciated in the story of Maine. Waldo's entrepreneurial efforts were reinvigorated by Henry Knox, who acquired much of Waldo's estate through his marriage to Lucy Flucker, Samuel Waldo's granddaughter. *Courtesy of Bowdoin College Museum of Art, Brunswick Maine, bequest of Mrs. Lucy Flucker Thatcher.*

recognition of his services. Within several years, Waldo, through purchase and legal action, had obtained 92 percent of the company's shares, and the Muscongus Patent became the Waldo Patent.[81]

Looking to exploit his newly acquired holdings in midcoast Maine, Waldo actively encouraged the reestablishment of the communities east of Pemaquid. In 1735, forty-seven families of Scots-Irish descent assumed residence along the banks of the St. George River in present Thomaston and Warren.[82] Although the area had been devoid of settlers since the destruction of the fledgling community of Lincoln thirteen years before, the presence of the truck house and St. George's fort provided a foundation and sense of security for the new easternmost settlement in Maine. Waldo envisioned St. George as the hub of a bustling commercial fiefdom capitalizing on the area's tremendous natural resources. Trading in land, timber products and lime, Waldo hoped to expand his already considerable personal wealth and establish himself as a member of colonial America's landed gentry. In 1742, Waldo established the community of Broad Bay (Waldoboro). Unlike the Scots-Irish settlers of St. George, many of whom previously resided elsewhere on the Maine or New Hampshire frontier, the new residents of Broad Bay hailed directly from Palatinate Germany. Like the community of St. George, Waldo founded Broad Bay as a commercial venture to further his social and financial ambitions. Unfortunately for Waldo and the residents of his coastal Maine dominion, the outbreak of King George's War would undermine the region's prospect for prosperity.

News of renewed war between France and England reached Cape Breton and the fortified French port of Louisbourg on May 3, 1744. Precipitated by Queen Maria Theresa's assumption of the Austrian throne in 1740, the War of Austrian Succession had, for the past four years, embroiled Europe's major powers in a contest over the continent's balance of power. Britain and France initially avoided direct conflict, but in March 1744, the two nations officially declared war. Receiving the announcement of war ahead of Massachusetts, French officials at Louisbourg seized the initiative by launching attacks against Nova Scotia. On May 24, French forces seized the English fishing station and garrison at Canso on the northeast tip of Nova Scotia. Offering no resistance to the French attack, the garrison and the community's inhabitants were sent back to Louisbourg as prisoners of war. Upon arrival at Louisbourg, the prisoners discovered that the impressive façade presented by the massive stone walls and bastions protecting the town belied its weakened condition. War in Europe had disrupted Louisbourg's lifeline of commerce and direct resupply by France. By the spring of 1744, the town's people were hungry, the walls were in disrepair and the garrison was on the verge of mutiny. Barely able to provide for the townspeople and the troops stationed there, French officials struggled to provide for the captives taken at Canso. To help ease the strain on the town's store of provisions, the citizens and soldiers seized at Canso were paroled and returned to Boston in September 1744 with tidings of the conditions at Louisbourg.

Further attacks were carried out against Nova Scotia in the wake of the assault on Canso. Annapolis Royal, the capital of Nova Scotia, formerly known by the French as Port Royal, was besieged twice over the summer of 1744. Both sieges were broken by the timely arrival of reinforcements from Massachusetts. Notably, operating alongside the armed Acadians and French forces from Louisbourg who participated in the attacks were several hundred Cape Sable and St. John's Indians. The presence of native warriors among the French suggested that the conflict would not remain confined to the European colonial powers but would engulf the region's native people as well, igniting latent tensions along the eastern frontier.

In addition to efforts against Canso and Annapolis Royal, French privateers (privately owned, government-sanctioned commerce raiders) set sail against the English commercial fleet during the spring and summer of 1744. Operating out of Louisburg and ports in Martinique and Guadalupe, they effectively disrupted New England merchant and fishing endeavors from the Grand Banks to the West Indies. In June alone, two privateers out of Louisbourg seized nine New England fishing vessels and a large merchantman coming from Ireland.[83] Despite early French successes, New England–sponsored privateers and the Massachusetts warship *Prince of Orange* quickly turned the tide against their French adversaries. By the end of June, Massachusetts had sent no fewer than fifteen privateers to sea, while the Quakers of Rhode Island and Pennsylvania provided twenty-three and eight privateer vessels, respectively.[84] By the end of the summer, New England vessels had reclaimed the Grand Banks, the Gulf of St. Lawrence and the Gulf of Maine.

Realizing war with France would inevitably lead to the resumption of hostilities with the Northeast's native people, Massachusetts began to bolster the defenses of the eastern frontier during the spring of 1744. In May and June, Massachusetts enacted legislation effectively putting the province on a war footing. The General Court authorized money for the repair of fortifications, passed laws for the levying of soldiers and established the number of men allocated to each of the garrisons on the eastern frontier. St. George's fort, the easternmost outpost, which lay within eyesight of

Penobscot territory, had its complement raised to forty men and officers. Fort Richmond, which stood on the doorstep of the lands claimed by the Kennebec, had twenty-five men earmarked for its defense, while Fort George at Brunswick and Fort Frederick at Pemaquid were allowed twelve and twenty-two soldiers, respectively.[85]

Although surprised by the timing of the French attacks in Nova Scotia, Massachusetts had been concerned for some time about the prospect of the war in Europe spreading to the colonies. The preceding winter, Governor William Shirley had ordered Captain Jabez Bradbury of St. George's fort to assess the attitudes of the Penobscot and gain their assurances of peace while reminding them of their obligations under Dummer's Treaty. As the truck master and military commander of St. George's fort, Bradbury was Massachusetts's primary diplomatic representative to the Penobscot people. He had previously served as a soldier on the Maine frontier during Dummer's War and had briefly acted as the truck master at Fort Richmond before assuming command of St. George's fort in 1742. During his tenure at St. George, Bradbury earned the trust and respect of the Penobscot people, who viewed him as a forthright diplomat and honest trader. In late June 1744, Bradbury reported to Governor Shirley that the Penobscot "had very lately been advised by St. John's Indians to draw off from their Village to some more remote part, & advised us in these parts to be constantly on our Guard."[86] Bradbury further indicated his belief in the Penobscot's peaceful intentions and their willingness to provide intelligence of impending attacks but cautioned, "There is at present all the appearance of friendship toward us, both in word and behavior that can be, But they are not to be trusted, and it's my opinion that the French will once more set them against us notwithstanding all that the Government can or will do."[87]

In an ongoing effort to manage the emerging crisis on the Maine frontier, Massachusetts continued to confer with the leadership of Piqwacket, Kennebec and Penobscot people over the summer and early fall of 1744. Throughout the course of the exchanges, Massachusetts regularly employed the proverbial carrot and stick approach in its effort to garner assurances of peace from the region's native people. The use of the stick to motivate the native people toward peaceful coexistence with their white neighbors was hardly necessary. Predominantly, Maine's resident native population wished to weather the impending storm by remaining neutral or by offering tacit support to Massachusetts. The greatest threat to security for all people in Maine came from the more militant factions of the eastern tribes residing in the French mission villages of Canada; fearful, belligerent Scots-Irish settlers; and a reactionary Massachusetts government.

On October 20, 1744, Massachusetts, in response to native participation in the attacks against Annapolis Royal and several other incidents of violence against whites in Nova Scotia, declared war against the Cape Sable and St. John's Indians. Addressing the native people of Maine who had granted their acquiescence to Dummer's Treaty, the Penobscot in particular, Governor Shirley stated within the declaration of war, "I do hereby…require the said Friend Indians agreeable to their solemn Treaty with this Governm$^t$ to join us in this war with the Cape Sables & S$^t$ John's Indians & to pursue them as Enemies & Rebels."[88]

Traveling to St. George in November, Colonel William Pepperell of Kittery informed the Penobscot of the declaration of war and demanded the Penobscot furnish Massachusetts with warriors in accordance with Dummer's Treaty. Given forty days to comply, the Penobscot were informed of Massachusetts's intentions to declare war against them should they fail to fulfill their treaty obligations.

The moment of truth was at hand for the Penobscot people, many of whom seemed to have desired nothing more than to remain uninvolved in the unfolding crisis. Massachusetts's declaration of war against the Cape Sable and St. John's Indians and subsequent demands for Penobscot support effectively forced war upon them in the autumn of 1744. The Penobscot were presented with no good options. Internal factionalism and divided opinion likely precluded any substantive decision. No matter the course they pursued, the ultimate outcome would be the resumption of war. The only question was which enemy they would face. If they chose passive neutrality or aligned themselves with their eastern neighbors, the Penobscot would again endure war with Massachusetts and their white neighbors. If they upheld their treaty obligations to Massachusetts, they would continue to receive the benefits of ongoing material support through the truck house at St. George but invariably be subjected to attack by other native people, suffer the humiliation of surrendering their sovereignty and likely sow the seeds of their own internal conflict. In January, the chief sagamores of the Penobscot responded to Massachusetts's ultimatum. In their reply, they stated "that their young men would not comply with the proposal of taking up arms against the St. John's Indians, their brethren."[89] The answer provided by the Penobscot is interesting. It either accurately reflects generational divisions within the tribe, or it is a subtle diplomatic evasion meant to project a good faith effort on the part of Penobscot leadership in the hopes of maintaining neutrality while avoiding a full commitment to the terms of Dummer's Treaty.

Rather than declaring war as Pepperell predicted in November, Massachusetts remained agreeable to further intercourse with the Penobscot. Although casual ties between natives and whites were curtailed, trade through the truck houses remained open, as did the prospect for diplomatic conciliation. In a letter to Jabez Bradbury at St. George, Massachusetts summarized its position toward the Penobscot. While advising the fort commander and truck master to remain vigilant and prevent his soldiers and officers from "holding a Correspondence, or having Conversation of any kind with them,"[90] he was, regarding trade, further instructed to "prudently deal out in such manner as may make the Indians continue their Dependence."[91] In the same letter, Massachusetts advised Bradbury of a planned expedition against Louisbourg and implored him to squelch any rumors of the operation among the local population lest the natives and, by extension, the French learn of the proposed attack.

Governor William Shirley first proposed seizing the fortified town of Louisburg to the General Court of Massachusetts on January 9, 1744/45. Although Shirley firmly embraced the notion of taking the port town, the original idea was not his own. It is not entirely clear who first proposed the idea to Shirley. Likely there were several proponents of the attack who garnered Shirley's attention. Historians have long identified John Bradstreet, who went on to serve with distinction as a British officer during the French and Indian War, as a likely contributor to Shirley's plan. Bradstreet had been part of the Canso garrison when it was taken by the French in May 1744. As a prisoner of war held at Louisburg, Bradstreet saw firsthand the dire situation of the town's inhabitants, garrison and defenses. Deteriorating walls, insufficient ordnance, a mutinous garrison and a populace suffering from chronic food shortages all spoke to the town's vulnerability. Upon returning to Boston in September, Bradstreet and other members of the Canso garrison reported their observations to the government of Massachusetts and Governor Shirley himself.[92]

In November 1744, Shirley sent a letter of introduction for Captain Ryal, who had been an officer aboard a British sloop taken at Canso, to Governor

Benning Wentworth of New Hampshire. In the letter, Shirley indicated that Captain Ryal would "be of considerable service…from his particular knowledge of Louisburg, and of its harbour; and of the great consequences of the acquisition of Cape Breton."[93] Clearly, by this point in time, Shirley was beginning to formulate plans for the future expedition.

Maine merchant William Vaughn of Damariscotta was another early and outspoken advocate of an attack against Louisbourg. Vaughn came from a wealthy, influential New England family who earned their fortune in the fishing industry. When Vaughn graduated from Harvard College in 1722 at the age

John Bradstreet has long been credited as a contributor to Governor Shirley's plan to seize the French port of Louisbourg. During the siege, Bradstreet assumed operational command of William Pepperell's regiment. Bradstreet went on to serve with distinction as a British officer during the French and Indian War. *Courtesy of Wikimedia Commons.*

of nineteen, he was ranked third in his class at a time when class standing was determined not by academic achievement but by social standing.[94] During the 1720s, Vaughn capitalized on his family's wealth and experience in the lucrative fishing trade, establishing a fishing station on Matinicus Island. Vaughn expanded his entrepreneurial endeavors, founding a commercial enterprise exporting timber products, salmon, shad and alewives from his holdings in and around Damariscotta.[95] Throughout the 1730s and early 1740s, Vaughn prospered as a merchant and trader, developing ties with French merchant interests at Louisbourg. Whether Vaughn ever visited Louisbourg personally or if he obtained information about the fortress through his business associates is unclear. Beyond a doubt, Vaughn, like Bradstreet and Ryal, was well aware of Louisbourg's vulnerability when he approached Governor Shirley with a proposal to take the city by storm during the winter of 1744–45.

In his initial presentation to the General Court of Massachusetts regarding the possibility of raising an expedition against Louisbourg, Shirley indicated:

> *In the course of the present War the utmost annoyance of our Navigation and Trade in general, and the frequent captures of our provisions vessels, and the destruction of our Fishery in particular from the Harbour of Louisbourg, it is evident that nothing would more effectually promote the interest of this Province at this juncture than a reduction of that place…From the best information that can be had of the circumstances of the Town and the number of soldiers and Militia within it and of the situation of the Harbour, I have good reason to think that if Two Thousand men were landed upon the island as soon as may be conveniently got ready…such a number of men would…make themselves masters of the Town and Harbour.[96]*

Upon consideration of the cost involved in such an undertaking, the General Court turned down Shirley's proposition. Frustrated by the legislature's vote, a coalition of North Shore merchants with a vested interest in commercial shipping and the fishing industry petitioned the General Court to reconsider its decision. On January 26, the General Court, by a narrow margin, reversed its prior position and authorized expenditures for an expedition to take Louisburg.

With political and financial backing for the undertaking secured, Governor Shirley sent letters to the governors of New England's other colonies asking for support. New Hampshire, Connecticut and Rhode Island all vowed to contribute to the expedition. In addition to the 3,300 men raised by Massachusetts, New Hampshire contributed 304 men and officers, while Connecticut sent 516 soldiers on the condition that their own Roger Wolcott serve as the expedition's second in command.[97] Rhode Island, despite internal wrangling that delayed its recruitment efforts, did raise 150 men, but not before the army set sail for its intended target. New York pledged to contribute ten pieces of heavy artillery, and both New Jersey and Pennsylvania agreed to provide financial support for the undertaking.

Furnishing the preponderance of the men and assuming the lion's share of the financial burden for the operation, it fell to Massachusetts to appoint the army's commander. Having experienced two decades of peace, Massachusetts lacked an active military establishment from which to select a suitable candidate. Instead, as was often the case throughout the period, the government based its decision concerning military leadership on political considerations as opposed to martial experience. Possessing astute

William Shirley, governor of Massachusetts, presided over the government of Massachusetts throughout King George's War and the beginning of the French and Indian War. *Courtesy of Wikimedia Commons.*

political acumen, an extensive patronage web and a sound reputation as a businessman and member of the General Court, William Pepperell of Kittery was appointed to lead the expedition, holding the rank of major general in the Massachusetts provincial army. At his side, Massachusetts commissioned

Samuel Waldo as a brigadier general. Although Waldo possessed less tact than Pepperell, he was nonetheless a well-connected, influential member of the General Court and close personal associate of Governor William Shirley. Each commanding one of Maine's two militia regiments, Waldo and Pepperell, through their combined recruiting efforts, enlisted more than one thousand Maine men, nearly a third of the Massachusetts total, to take part in the Louisbourg expedition.

In addition to the land forces raised, the New England colonies assembled more than one hundred ships of varying sizes for the expedition. The majority of the ships were to be used as transports for the nearly four thousand men readied to take Louisbourg. Most of the transports were converted fishing vessels that had been moldering in port as a result of the depredation and fear caused by the activities of French privateers. To obtain the use of these vessels, Massachusetts contracted their hire and insured their owners against any losses. The New England colonies also contributed thirteen ships mounting 220 guns to protect the transports and support the army.[98] Fearing that this armed flotilla would prove inadequate in the event that a French fleet should arrive to relieve Louisbourg, Governor Shirley wrote to Commodore Peter Warren of the Royal Navy, then operating in and around Antigua, asking for support. Shirley had also dispatched a letter to the Duke of Newcastle, serving as the secretary of state and responsible for colonial affairs, requesting direct orders be issued to Warren for his participation in the operation against Louisburg. Initially, Warren deferred providing assistance per Shirley's request in the absence of orders from his superiors. After receiving a letter from the Duke of Newcastle, which he interpreted as orders to support Shirley, Warren set sail for the waters off Nova Scotia with three warships of the Royal Navy.

On March 24, 1745, the transports and makeshift warships of the Louisbourg expedition weighed anchor from Nantasket Roads bound eastward. After rendezvousing and regrouping at Townsend (Boothbay), the fleet sailed on to the rocky, wind-swept shores of Canso. The New England fleet arrived incrementally at Canso over the first week of April. Fog bound, anticipating the arrival of cannon from New York and waiting for the ice around Louisbourg to break up, the expedition spent three restless weeks at Canso. On March 23, the English frigate *Eltham*, which Warren had relieved from its duty escorting mast ships bound for England, appeared off Canso. The next day, Warren arrived with the sixty-four-gun ship of the line *Superbe* and two frigates of forty guns, the *Mermaid* and *Launceston*. With news of ice-free water around Louisbourg, the expedition embarked and appeared before its intended target on March 30.

Commodore Peter Warren provided assistance from the Royal Navy to the New England forces assembled for the siege of Louisbourg in 1745. The lighthouse and island battery of Louisbourg Harbor can be seen in the background of this portrait. *Courtesy of Wikimedia Commons.*

Pepperell landed his army at Gabarus Bay south of the city's fortifications with minimal French resistance. Believing his forces were insufficient to adequately defend Louisbourg's extensive defensive works, Du Chambon, the garrison's military commander, withdrew his troops to within the town's walls. Probing the hills west of the town, William Vaughn and the men under his command discovered that the French had abandoned the heavily fortified and strategically important outwork known as the Grand Battery. In their haste, the French had inadequately disabled the fortification's massive

This photo shows part of the extensive fortifications protecting the port town of Loiusburg on Cape Breton Island. In addition to the fort's massive walls, the picture features the building housing the governor's apartment, the chapel and the barracks of the king's bastion. *Courtesy of Wikimedia Commons.*

guns and failed to destroy much of the gunpowder and shot necessary for their operation. Turning the guns against their former owners, Vaughn commenced the bombardment and siege of Louisbourg. Over the next month and a half, the New England forces under Pepperell's command established a series of artillery positions ringing the town, from which they conducted a slow cannonade of Louisbourg. Commodore Warren became increasingly frustrated with the New Englanders' lack of progress in reducing the town as May turned into June. Several proposed attacks and joint operations between the New England ground forces and the Royal Navy were abandoned due to poor weather, colonial concerns about the feasibility of the undertakings and pervasive sickness among the ranks of the New Englanders. The one attack carried out by the New Englanders against a defensive work at the entrance of the harbor known as the Island Battery was repulsed with heavy losses.

Despite Warren's frustration with what he perceived to be the New England army's lack of resolve, the French were beginning to feel the strain of protracted siege. In late May, the French ship of the line *Vigilant*, which had been dispatched from France with reinforcements and provisions for Louisbourg, was intercepted by the combined English and New England fleet as it approached the shores of North America. By mid-June, Du Chambon had learned of the *Vigilant*'s seizure and was aware that Louisbourg would not receive relief, resupply or reinforcement. With all but one of the town's structures undamaged by Yankee bombardment, the town's inhabitants, hungry and fearing English depredations should the town be taken by storm, beseeched Du Chambon to capitulate. Isolated, faced with mounting civil discontent and with dwindling stocks of provisions and gunpowder, Du Chambon surrendered Louisburg to the combined English and New England forces on June 16, 1745. The next day, General Pepperell and Colonel John Bradstreet, who had assumed operational command of Pepperell's regiment, entered the city at the head of the New England army.

The reduction of Louisbourg proved to be a source of both great pride and discontent for New England, Massachusetts in particular. The men of the New England army had, in part, been enticed to serve with notions of being awarded shares of plunder upon the fall of the town. The articles of surrender negotiated at the conclusion of the siege acknowledged the sanctity of the French soldiers' and inhabitants' material possession, denying the men of New England what they perceived to be their rightful bounty. Meanwhile, the officers and sailors of the Royal Navy were awarded the spoils of war resulting from the seizure of the *Vigilant*. Chafing at English derision of their character and contributions to the expedition, New Englanders fostered a long-standing disdain for English arrogance and prerogative. As a source of pride, Louisbourg mobilized the people and institutions of New England to a degree never achieved previously. The expedition galvanized political and commercial interests while eliciting overpowering enthusiasm among the ordinary people, particularly in Maine, who provided the manpower making the enterprise possible.

Proportionately, Maine contributed more soldiers for the Louisbourg expedition than any other region of New England. Approximately one-quarter of the army that served at Cape Breton came from the communities of Maine. Of the estimated 2,855 men on the muster rolls of Maine's two militia regiments,[99] nearly 1,000—more than a third of those eligible for military service—are believed to have enlisted for the expedition.[100] With many men from the midcoast serving in Samuel Waldo's regiment before the walls of Louisbourg, the region was particularly vulnerable when war returned to the region during the summer of 1745.

Hostilities in Maine erupted on July 19, 1745, with an assault against the community and fort at St. George (Thomaston). While the fort was besieged, the war party, identified as consisting of Cape Sable and Canadian mission village Indians, set fire to one of the garrison houses sheltering the town's residents, burned homes, killed livestock and reduced a sawmill to ashes. Characteristically, after harassing the fort—seizing, in this case, one captive and destroying what they could of the community—the native party withdrew and disappeared into the Maine woods. Other attacks occurred across the region in the wake of the assault on St. George. Settlers at Pemaquid, New Meadows, Topsham and North Yarmouth were assailed, while a series of attacks, abductions and attempted abductions was subsequently carried out against the inhabitants in and around St. George.

On July 25, 1745, Massachusetts demanded the Penobscot and Norridgewock remit to their custody those of their people who had participated in the recent attack against St. George. Whether or not resident Penobscot or Norridgewock took part in the attack is open to debate. Some of the more militant factions within the tribes may have been present during the affair. However, it is equally likely that expatriate Penobscot and/or Norridgewock from the Canadian mission villages—over whom the resident sagamores had no control—carried out the attack. If the Penobscot and Norridgewock were unable to turn over the perpetrators, they were expected to provide sufficient hostages from among their people and provide Massachusetts with at least thirty warriors within fourteen days.[101] The government of Massachusetts went on to state, "If the said Penobscot and Norridgewock Tribes should refuse this, that his Excellency be Humbly moved to declare War against them, only giving liberty to such of them as shall be so inclined, to come and live with us, to be protected and subsisted by us; provided they come in within fourteen days after the Declaration of War."[102]

On August 23, having failed to deliver perpetrators, hostages or warriors, Massachusetts officially declared war against the Penobscot, the Norridgewock and all the native people of Maine.

On September 5, 1745, four Penobscot men approached the fort at St. George to conduct trade or negotiations with Captain Bradbury. Either the native party was unaware of the existing state of war, or more likely, they were taking advantage of the fourteen-day grace period to obtain a final, last-minute disbursement of provisions and trade goods from the truck house. After conferring with the Penobscot party, Bradbury sent them away from the fort, advising them of his inability to protect them from the actions of the local inhabitants who, little more than a month before, had witnessed the destruction of their homes and property at the hands of a native war party. Inexplicably, the natives failed to heed Bradbury's warning and encamped on the banks of the Mill River less than a mile from the fort. Motivated by fear, greed and anger, a posse of nineteen volunteers from the community at St. George, led by local militia leaders Captain Benjamin Burton and Lieutenant Proctor, fell upon the four Penobscot. During the ensuing attack, two of the native men, known to local whites as Colonel Morris and Captain Sam, were killed and scalped. One of the men managed to escape the vengeful clutches of the volunteers, while the final member of the party, Colonel Job, was taken prisoner and sent to Boston, where he died in captivity. Following the attack, the government of Massachusetts expressed concern about the propriety of the attack, and the application put forth by Burton and his men to redeem their scalp and captive bounties appears to have been rejected.[103]

Following attacks at Sheepscot and Topsham in which several men were killed and scalped while harvesting corn, Maine settled into a period of quiet tension spanning the autumn and winter of 1745 and 1746. Gorham experienced 1746's first wave of attacks on April 19 and 20, presaging a return of violence across the Maine frontier. Subsequent raids took place throughout May at St. George, Pemaquid, Sheepscot, North Yarmouth and Falmouth. The largest attack of 1746 occurred at Broad Bay (Waldoboro). At the time of the attack, most of Broad Bay's German inhabitants were living within the protective confines of the several fortified garrisons scattered across the settlement. Their isolated farm homesteads lay vacant and vulnerable. During the early morning hours of May 21, a native war party attacked the garrisons while simultaneously killing livestock and burning abandoned homes. While the garrisons withstood the assault, the war party managed to breech the palisade fence surrounding the community's meetinghouse where several families sought shelter. Seizing some occupants as captives and killing and scalping others, the attackers set the church ablaze.[104] Retiring with their captives, the war party left the community terrified, grief stricken and demoralized. Unable to adequately provide shelter and sustenance for themselves, many of the town's residents sought safety and security elsewhere.

Like the inhabitants of Broad Bay, many residents of the eastern settlements already had, or soon would, abandon their homes. The communities from the St. George to the Sheepscot Rivers became shells of their former selves. Broad Bay was committed to ashes, Townsend (Boothbay) was deserted and St. George's became a skeleton community. Seeking refuge in Massachusetts and the Scots-Irish communities of New Hampshire, many families sought to escape the fear, uncertainty and hardship of war on the midcoast. Those who chose to remain did so enclosed within the region's palisaded garrisons, leaving their homes and fields empty and untended.

Rumors of a French attempt to retake Acadia contributed to the fear precipitating the exodus from the midcoast. In June 1746, a French fleet of seventy warships and transports departed the port of Brest carrying more than three thousand soldiers.[105] The fleet was dispatched to North America to reclaim Louisburg and threaten English interests from Nova Scotia to Boston with the assistance of armed French Acadians and native allies. In early September, Governor Shirley, in a speech before the General Court, added to the near state of panic gripping Maine, proclaiming:

> *There were probably in all Nova Scotia a mixed population...consisting of French Acadians, French and Natives...who could furnish six thousand able to bear arms and take the field; and only waited a favorable or safe opportunity...if these were joined by the great body of Indians at Penobscot and Kennebec, they would under the auspices of the French...overrun the eastern Provinces and New Hampshire.*[106]

Within days of Shirley's speech, the French fleet arrived at Chebucto (Halifax), Nova Scotia. During the three-month passage between Brest and the shores of North America, the soldiers and sailors aboard ship were ravaged by disease. By the time the fleet put in at Chebucto, 1,270 men had perished at sea, and a further 1,130 died upon arrival, precluding any sort of campaign against Louisbourg, Nova Scotia or New England.[107] Cape Sable and St. John's Indians who greeted the French in anticipation of supporting their operations were introduced to the disease endemic among the French. Unwittingly bringing the pathogen or pathogens back to their own people, it is estimated that perhaps as many as a third of the tribes' populations succumbed to the disease over 1746 and 1747.[108]

Spared the anticipated onslaught of the French and Indians over the fall of 1746, the inhabitants of midcoast Maine awaited the resumption of raids that would surely commence with the arrival of spring. Throughout April and May 1747, Pemaquid, Damariscotta, Newcastle and Sheepscot were subjected to a series of particularly costly raids. On April 27, as many as thirty men, women and children were killed or taken captive in a wave of attacks up and down the Damariscotta River.[109] Subsequent attacks occurred in the area over early May, resulting in the deaths and seizure of several more inhabitants. On May 22, a group of men fishing for alewives was attacked, leaving fourteen men dead, including three soldiers from Fort Frederick. Four days later, the fort itself was assailed by more than one hundred attackers. The assault, although having no effect on the fort itself, left ten soldiers—five from the fort and five belonging to a detachment from Casco Bay—dead.[110]

Later in the summer of 1747, another force, this time consisting of both French and Indians, made its appearance along the coast of Maine. On the morning of September 1, the war party surprised a detachment of soldiers outside the walls of Pemaquid's Fort Frederick. Three Massachusetts soldiers were killed in the ambush, while two more were scalped and left for dead. Having been alerted to the attackers' presence, the fort's garrison easily withstood the two-hour attack that followed.[111] Unable to take the fort, the assailants shifted their attention eastward to St. George. As they had during Dummer's War twenty-five years earlier, the besiegers attempted to undermine and blow up the walls of St. George's fort using subterraneous approaches. Just as had happened previously, the attackers' efforts were frustrated by the collapse of the tunnels under heavy rains.[112] Failing to seize either Fort Frederick or St. George's fort, the French and Indian war party splintered, conducting a series of isolated raids against civilian targets of opportunity across the region. As had become the cycle of warfare on the frontier, attacks subsided by the end of September as the people of Maine, native and white alike, prepared for the onset of winter.

The communities of the eastern frontier were beset by extreme hardship over the winter of 1747–48. The effects of mass emigration, the destruction of livestock by native marauders, reduced crop yields due to poor weather conditions, the constraints imposed by garrison life and war-related declines in timber-related exports all contributed to the adversity beleaguering midcoast Maine. Rampant inflation incidental to the voluminous creation of unsecured paper money to finance the Louisbourg expedition further exacerbated the developing economic and subsistence crisis. By the end of the war, prices for goods paid in Massachusetts currency more than doubled, adding to the despair of the cash-strapped, import-dependent people of the midcoast.[113] The native people of Maine also suffered throughout the winter of 1747–48. Like their white neighbors, the native people of Maine were experiencing food shortages caused by the disruptions of war, drought and unusually severe winter weather. Deprived of trade with the English for nearly two years, the people of the eastern tribes were confronted by acute material distress and privation. By the spring of 1748, both sides were near their breaking points.

In July 1748, news of a preliminary peace between England and France reached North America. Aside from several small-scale attacks conducted against inhabitants in and around Brunswick and North Yarmouth (Yarmouth, Freeport, Harpswell) in May, the Maine frontier remained relatively quiet over the spring and summer of 1748. In early October, Penobscot leaders approached Captain Jabez Bradbury at St. George's fort requesting peace talks with Massachusetts. William Lithgow at Fort Richmond was likewise beseeched with requests for negotiations by Norridgewock representatives. For nearly a year, Massachusetts and the sagamores of the eastern tribes worked to establish a formal end to the war in Maine. Finally, on October 16, 1749, peace was officially restored with the ratification of the Treaty of Falmouth. Signed by nineteen sagamores and chief leaders of the Penobscot, Norridgewock, St. Francis and Becancour Indians, the treaty merely reaffirmed Dummer's Treaty signed twenty-four years previously. Just as they had before, the eastern tribes agreed to allow development of the former English settlements, to support Massachusetts militarily in the event of future conflict and to address all grievances with their white neighbors through the courts of Massachusetts.

Over the winter of 1748–49, as Massachusetts and the eastern tribes worked to reestablish peace in Maine, news of renewed peace between France and Great Britain reached the governments of New France and New England. In October 1748, after more than six months of negotiations, Britain and France signed the Treaty of Aix-la-Chapelle concluding the War of Austrian Succession. To the astonishment of the people and governments of New England, the treaty returned Cape Breton and the fortified port of Louisbourg to the French. Having organized and executed the largest and most successful colonial military undertaking to date, the people of Massachusetts were outraged by Britain's disregard for their expenditure of men, money and material in taking Louisbourg. Concerns in North America were not at the forefront of British diplomatic efforts at the end of the War of Austrian Succession. The Treaty of Aix-la-Chapelle allowed Britain to extricate itself from a continental conflict not proceeding in its favor, and Louisbourg was bargained away as a political expediency. France walked away from the war and negotiating table with the upper hand. Emboldened by its successes, France would, in the near future, more vigorously pursue its interests on the frontiers of North America.

Materially, nothing changed on the Maine frontier in the wake of King George's War. The Treaties of Falmouth and Aix-la-Chapelle returned all that was fought for, gained and lost to the status quo of pre-1744. Unlike preceding conflicts, Massachusetts did not conduct any large-scale offensives against the people and villages of the eastern tribes, choosing instead to fight a predominantly defensive war. Governor Shirley did propose pushing the Maine frontier eastward through the construction of a fort and truck house at the head of Penobscot Bay, which would have required a substantial military operation as it entailed the seizure and occupation of a considerable part of the Penobscot's homelands. Unwilling to make such a military and financial commitment, the General Court of Massachusetts rejected Shirley's proposal, and the eastern boundary between Massachusetts and the Penobscot remained fixed at St. George.

As in all other conflicts, the native people of Maine suffered tremendously. War had been thrust upon them by forces beyond their control. In the end, seeking to reestablish trade and physical security, the native people agreed to a peace treaty that all but stripped them of their sovereignty and autonomy. Failing to adequately address the concerns and issues facing the people of the eastern frontier, the Treaty of Falmouth established a truce rather than a lasting peace.

# Chapter 6
## *Justice*

The ink had barely dried on the recently signed Treaty of Falmouth before the agreement was torn asunder. Within weeks of the treaty, the people of Maine were once again confronted with the very real possibility of renewed conflict. Stemming from a violent and unprovoked encounter between natives and whites at Wiscasset, developments over 1749 and 1750 would test both sides' commitment to peace in the aftermath of King George's War. Like preceding peace agreements, the Treaty of Falmouth prohibited acts of revenge, stipulating:

> *If any Controversy or Difference at any time hereafter happen to arise between any of the English and Indians, for any real or supposed wrong or injury done on either side, no private Revenge shall be taken for the same but proper Application shall be made to his Majesty's Government upon the place for Remedy and Redress thereof, in a due Course of Justice: We submitting ourselves to be Ruled and Governed by his Majesty's Laws, and desiring to have the Benefit of the same.*[114]

The Wiscasset incident would try the native people's patience with the English legal system and undermine their faith in Massachusetts's commitment to upholding treaty obligations. It also underscored many of the prevailing attitudes and cultural predispositions of the region's predominantly Scots-Irish population.

On December 2, 1749, a band of fifteen natives with family ties to the Norridgewock, Penobscot, St. Francis and Becancour communities encamped approximately one mile upriver from Wiscasset. Overnight, they were unexpectedly attacked by a band of local inhabitants from the nearby village. Although the particulars of the incident have been lost to time, the late-night encounter left chief Hegen (known by English speakers as Saccary Harry) dead and two others, Andrew and Captain Job, critically wounded. Fleeing the scene, the survivors made their way by canoe via the Sheepscot and Sasanoa Rivers to Parkers Island (Georgetown) to report the crime. On December 6, two women, one of whom was Hegen's widow, lodged a formal complaint with Major Samuel Denny, the lower Kennebec's chief civil magistrate and justice of the peace. Upon receiving the complaint, Denny summoned Deputy Sheriff Captain Samuel Harnden and issued a warrant for the arrest of the assailants.

News of the attack percolated through the community at Wiscasset in the days following the affair. Arriving at Wiscasset on December 7, Denny and Harnden were accosted by a crowd intent on obstructing the apprehension of the alleged perpetrators. With faces blackened to obscure their identities, the assembled rabble assaulted Harnden and Denny. During the ensuing scuffle, sixty-year-old Denny, the chief representative of Massachusetts authority in the region, was thrown to the ground. Despite the vigilante efforts of the mob to protect the individuals responsible for the attack, Harnden managed to arrest all but one of the suspects. Obadiah Albee Jr., the chief suspect and supposed ringleader of the incident, had previously slipped away from Wiscasset aboard a schooner bound for Massachusetts. Although Albee avoided apprehension, Samuel Ball, Benjamin Ledite, Richard Brown, Unity Brown, Richard Holbrook and Benjamin Holbrook, all of Wiscasset, were subsequently taken into custody.

Of the men suspected of perpetrating the attack, only Albee, Ball and Ledite were actually indicted for the crimes of murder and assault with the intention to kill.[115] Benjamin and Richard Holbrook were each put under a fifty-pound bond to appear as witnesses in the case, while Unity and Richard Brown were released altogether. On December 15, 1749, Harnden, with Ball and Ledite in custody, set off for the county seat at York, where the two prisoners were to be confined in jail awaiting trial.

En route to York, Harnden secured overnight accommodations for himself, his assistants and the detainees in Falmouth at the house of John Thoms (near present Morrills Corner in Portland). Overnight, Ball and Ledite escaped from the house and Harnden's watch with the assistance of a sympathetic mob that broke into the house, liberating the two detainees.[116]

York County Jail. Samuel Ball and Benjamin Ledite, two of the perpetrators of the "Wiscasset incident," were held here under the guard of nine men over the winter of 1749–50. *Author's photo.*

Immediately following their escape, reports of Ball and Ledite being sheltered in Gorham led authorities to conduct a house-by-house, building-by-building search of the entire community, to no avail. On December 26, 1749, a reward of fifty pounds was promised for the apprehension of each fugitive. A twenty-five-pound reward was also offered for anyone aiding their escape. In the advertisement proclaiming the reward, Ball was described as "a man of middling stature with a full eye of a light complexion, he wears his own hair, he had on a blue cloth jacket, blue stockings, an old hat and trousers; he has lately been seen with a frock over his jacket."[117]

Evading capture for nearly three weeks, Ball and Ledite were finally apprehended by Captain Jonathan Bean of the Saco blockhouse (Dayton) and committed to the York County Jail on January 10, 1749/50. Amid concerns of another mob attempt to set the two men free, authorities established a nine-man guard to secure the suspects.

While his co-conspirators were on the run in Maine, Obadiah Albee was arrested in Massachusetts. On December 21, 1749, the schooner on which

Albee fled put into port at Marblehead. Learning of the reward offered for Albee's capture, the vessel's captain alerted local authorities to his presence among his crew. To Albee's detriment, he had admitted to his part in the attack, boasting to his shipmates how he "snapped his gun" at the native party.[118] Seizing Albee, officials initially held him at the Essex County Jail in Salem, from which he was later transferred to the York County Jail with his co-conspirators.

Cognizant of the inflammatory nature of the case, Massachusetts officials convened a special court session to hear it in late February 1749/50. In the months following the attack at Wiscasset, Massachusetts collected evidence and assembled witnesses in its case against Ball, Ledite and Albee. Over the winter, officials raised concerns about the difficulties posed by assembling the necessary jury, judges, lawyers and witnesses to hear the case. Their concerns proved prescient, as one of the judges scheduled to attend the session was forced to excuse himself from the proceedings due to illness. Unable to secure another judge for the hearing, the trial was postponed until the regular session of the York County court in June.

Unmet expectations for a timely execution of justice caused worry and frustration along the frontier. In early April, Jabez Bradbury at St. George expressed concern regarding the trial's delay, stating, "Its my opinion if there is not speedy satisfaction Given to the Indians on that account it may be attended with ill Consequences."[119] Over the spring, both Bradbury and William Lithgow at Fort Richmond heard the complaints of the native people. Loron of the Penobscot proclaimed to Bradbury, "We have waited patiently...and as you told we should have justice done us, so we expect you will really do it."[120] Chief Asserremo of the Worenock (Wawenock) was more direct than Loron when he conferred with Bradbury, declaring:

> We have waited a long time Expecting that you would do us Justice agreeable to yᵉ promise you then made at Casco now Brother we and our young men would have you be Quick in putting those murderers to Death within a months time to cover the blood that now lyes on the ground which we are Desirous may be covered or else all will not be well.[121]

On June 9, 1750, the York County court convened to hear the Massachusetts Bay Colony's case against Obadiah Albee Jr. Massachusetts committed substantial financial resources to gathering evidence, securing witnesses and preparing its case in anticipation of the high-profile trial. Albee, the supposed ringleader in the attack, was charged with the murder of Chief Hegen of Norridgewock and Becancour. In accordance with Massachusetts law, Albee was awarded the benefit of a trial before his peers. Despite the best attempts of Massachusetts prosecutors, the jury delivered a not guilty verdict on June 12. Court officials were shocked by the verdict. Writing in his journal, Parson Smith of Falmouth noted, "Albee was acquitted to the great surprise of the court. This unhappy affair gives the country an ill name, and it is feared will bring on war."[122] Equally astonishing, the cases against Samuel Ball and Benjamin Ledite were not heard at all while the York County court was in session due to concerns over the partiality of the jury.

Fearing reprisals, Massachusetts attempted to assuage the anger of native people by reaching out to the aggrieved families. In the immediate aftermath of the Wiscasset attack, Massachusetts, through the agency of Samuel Denny, William Lithgow and Jabez Bradbury, had made concerted efforts to care for and honor the victims of the attack. Shortly after reporting the incident, the survivors were conveyed to St. George, where they received sustenance and gifts over the winter. In the wake of Albee's verdict, Massachusetts stepped up efforts to effect rapprochement with the offended families and, by extension, the people of the eastern tribes. In July, Lieutenant Governor Spencer Phips invited the victims of the attack, their families and tribal leaders to confer with him in Boston. For several days in early August, the native delegation responding to Phips's invitation was plied with food, drink and platitudes of peace. Gifts of shirts, blankets, hats, stockings, a kettle and money were distributed to the attendees as remuneration for their losses and damaged honor. Receiving the diplomatic courtesies of Lieutenant Governor Phips, the families and their representatives returned to their homes in Maine seemingly satisfied with the indulgences of Massachusetts.

The diplomatic efforts of Massachusetts over the summer of 1750 proved ineffective in quieting tensions on the Maine frontier. On August 2, 1750, as Massachusetts was courting the native dignitaries in Boston, Thomas Fletcher, the second in command at St. George's fort, dispatched a letter to Lieutenant Governor Phips reporting intelligence of a looming attack against the midcoast. In his letter, Fletcher indicated, "There are 60 Indians from Kenedy [Canada] at penobscott come with full purpose to take this fort, burn and destroy the whole settlem$^{nt}$ on this Rever."[123] Phips, realizing the gravity of the situation, issued orders to the region's garrison commanders to be on alert for impending attacks. On September 7, Jabez Bradbury, receiving additional intelligence, advised the commander of the Pemaquid garrison:

*Sir this Day I am informed that Seventy Indians ar gon from penapscot in order to fall on y* people at Sheepsgut; I think that you Inform them of their Danger as soon as posible they tell me y* the people on this Side Damarscotey are Safe & that none will hurt them, the above mentioned Indians ar from Canady, the ponapscots are Still Disirous of Living peasably with us.*[124]

Although Bradbury's intelligence was good, it came too late to mount an effective response.

James Whidden and his family had been living on Swan Island for less than a year. Having served as an officer during the Louisbourg campaign, Whidden moved to the island with his wife; his two sons; his daughter; her husband, Lazarus Noble; their seven children; and two domestic servants following King George's War. Despite rumors and warnings of impending raids, the Whidden family had not sought shelter in one of the region's garrisons, as had many of the area's inhabitants. Isolated and exposed in their home on Swan Island, the family was easy prey for the war party of which Bradbury warned.

In the early morning hours of September 8, 1750, a band of native assailants fell upon the unsuspecting Whidden family. Hiding in the cellar of their home, Mr. Whidden and his wife escaped the notice of the native intruders. However, the rest of the family, including seven children between six months and fourteen years of age, were seized as captives. After plundering the house, the war party departed with their prize of thirteen men, women and children. While one body of natives attacked the Noble and Whidden family, another laid siege to Fort Richmond for nearly three hours. Although they made no impression on the fort itself, the war party killed cattle and destroyed nearby property. Seizing one captive, Philip Jenkins, from the vicinity of the fort, the war party retreated up the Kennebec River and into the shadows of the Maine woods.

The next day, the war party vented its anger against Sheepscot just north of Wiscasset. William Ross and his son John were taken captive during the attack while several abandoned homes were burned and cattle killed. On September 10, the war party made an appearance in the Brunswick/Topsham area, where it again killed cattle, destroyed property and seized a young man, John Martin, as a captive. The spate of attacks left the inhabitants of the midcoast in a state of fear and uncertainty. On September 26, residents from Brunswick to Damariscotta signed a petition addressed to Lieutenant Governor Phips in which they described their plight:

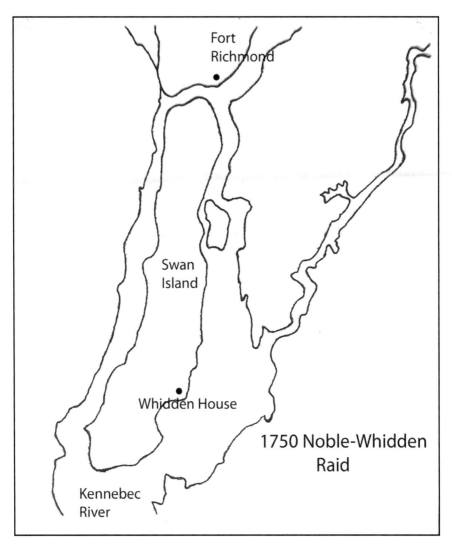

In 1750, during a supposed period of peace, thirteen members of the Noble and Whidden families were seized as captives and brought back to Canada. The raid was in retaliation for an unprovoked attack against a group of native people shortly after King George's War. *Author's map.*

*We the Subscribers for ourselves & in behalf of the Rest of the Inhabitants on the Frontiers of the Eastern Parts—*
*Humbly Show*
    *The poor distressed Condition that our part of the Country is in at present for we have had Seventeen People carried away Captive by the*

*Indians, two wounded & another mortally wounded which we suppose to be dead before this Time, One Garryson & likewise several Houses and Hay in the marshes burned & other Houses Rifled, Great Numbers of Cattle & Hogs killed, which has put our People in so much Fear that we cannot go from one Garrison to another without going by night, neither are we able with safety to gather in our Crops & if we lose our Crops we cannot live there this winter for want of Support for our Families.*[125]

In response, Massachusetts authorized raising 150 soldiers to be posted from Saco to St. George until November 1. By October, tensions were beginning to abate on the Maine frontier. Both William Lithgow at Fort Richmond and Jabez Bradbury at St. George's fort reported the Indians had slaked their thirst for vengeance during September's attacks. On October 10, 1750, Bradbury wrote to Lieutenant Governor Phips:

*Yesterday Came in here two of the Penobscots and this Day Came Squadook, they tell me the Indians that Took the People at Swan island and other Parts, are gon of Satisfied, having as they Say Paid themselves for the Mischeif done them at Wiscasset, and will hurt us no more. The Prisners are well on their way to Cannada being met by Som of the Penobscots on their Return from thence.*[126]

The fates of the captives taken during the raids of 1750 deserve particular note as they boldly illustrate the nature of mourning war as practiced by the native people of the Northeast. Not only was the attack at Wiscasset and the subsequent travesty of justice an affront to the honor, dignity and sovereignty of the region's native people, but the murder of Hegen and the crippling wounds suffered by Andrew and Job also precipitated economic hardship for their kinship bands through the loss of their productive value to the community. With kinship ties to Norridgewock, St. Francis and Becancour, the symbolic and material losses cut through several villages, making the need for compensatory justice that much more compelling.[127]

Of the seventeen captives taken during the raids of September 1750, thirteen—including the four oldest Noble children and all but one of the adults—were sold directly to the French for ready cash. Purchased by French seigneurs as laborers or domestic servants, all were eventually ransomed or returned home as the result of prisoner exchanges with the exception of Philip Jenkins, who died during captivity. Solomon Whidden, one of James Whidden's two sons, was held in servitude by his native captors. Escaping from his native masters, Solomon made his way to Quebec. There, Marquis de la Jonquiere, governor general of Quebec, refused to return him to his captors and granted him permission to work as a free man in Quebec. Unfortunately, Solomon died of disease in November 1750. Six-month-old Abigail Noble was adopted by her native captors and remained at Becancour, never to return to Maine or her family of origin. Like Abigail, Joseph Noble, who was eight years old when taken from Swan Island, never returned to his family. After residing with a native family at St. Francis, he was sold to and adopted by a French family. Francis (Fanny) Noble was two when she was adopted by a wealthy French family and renamed Eleanor. With her new family, Eleanor was afforded the comforts of wealth and prestige, including a classical education at a Montreal convent. Thirteen years later, Eleanor was ripped from her life of privilege and the only family she remembered and forced to return to her family on Swan Island as Fanny Noble.[128]

Although retribution was exacted and the hatchet buried for Albee's acquittal in the murder of Hegen, native communities awaited the execution of justice in Massachusetts's case against Samuel Ball and Benjamin Ledite. Concerned by the prospects of obtaining an impartial jury to hear their cases in Maine, Massachusetts sought alternative venues for the proceedings. Bills were put forward to move the trials to Middlesex County and later to Sussex County in Boston over the summer of 1750. However, the General Court of Massachusetts rejected the proposals, and the trials were held over until the next session of the York County court the following June. Meanwhile, Ball and Ledite remained confined to the York County Jail. In March 1751, Samuel Ball escaped from the jail and from all appearances was never apprehended to stand trial for his role in the 1749 assault in Wiscasset.[129]

When the York County Superior Court reconvened in June 1751, Benjamin Ledite stood before the court on two indictments. On the first count of "being present with Albee aiding and abetting in the murder of Hegen," Ledite was found not guilty.[130] On the second count of "assault on Job and Andrew with intent to kill, having a gun charged with powder which he did discharge and shoot at Job and Andrew, and did maliciously shoot Andrew in the left part of the back with a bullet, and wounded him grievously, and Job in the right groin with two swan shot, so that their lives were despaired of";[131] the jury found Benjamin Ledite guilty. Having established his guilt, the jury immediately passed sentence, proclaiming "that you Benjamin Ledite sit on the gallows with a rope about your neck one hour, and be whipt under the gallows twenty stripes on the naked back, and stand bound to keep the peace three years in the sum of £100, and pay the costs."[132]

The extent to which Ledite's public humiliation, corporal punishment and financial promise of civility satisfied the families of Hegen, Job and Andrew in unclear. Just prior to Ledite's trial, a series of native raids originating from the French mission villages spread panic from Casco Bay to St. George. The largest of these raids was conducted against a work party in the vicinity of the New Meadows River in today's Bath/Brunswick area. One man was killed and six were taken captive during the attack. The next day, two boys were seized in nearby North Yarmouth (Yarmouth, Freeport and Harpswell). The previous year, French officials, disappointed in resident Penobscot and Norridgewock outrage over Albee's acquittal, had pushed the more militant factions of those people residing in exile at St. Francis and Becancour into action with promises of material support for expeditions against the Maine frontier.[133] Likely the attacks of May and June 1751 were also encouraged by French instigation and not by local natives seeking justice through retribution. However, following the delivery of the jury's verdict in Ledite's case, the raids ceased, and peace talks between Massachusetts and the resident people of Maine commenced.

In late August 1751, Massachusetts delegates and representatives of peace-inclined Penobscot and Norridgewock factions met at St. George. Notably absent from the talks were envoys from the more militant factions of Maine's native people residing in Canada. Although the native attendees pledged their commitment to peace and ending the raids, Massachusetts remained skeptical of their ability to fulfill these promises without the endorsement of the mission village factions. Despite Massachusetts's concerns, the Maine frontier remained quiet over the next year. During the summer of 1752, Massachusetts reached out to all the principal Indian villages, including St. Francis and Becancour, to broker a more comprehensive peace plan for Maine. In October 1752, another conference was held at St. George with all major factions in attendance. No mention was made concerning the English failure of justice in the recent outbreak of violence during the talks. Rather, Massachusetts pointed out the native people's failure to uphold their treaty obligations and blamed them for "killing and captivating" settlers and "committing other acts of hostility."[134] As had become customary, the talks ended with the re-ratification of previous peace understandings. Although peace was officially restored in Maine as a result of the conference, no progress was made toward addressing any of the issues propelling the cycle of perpetual conflict.

# Chapter 7

## *Parallels*

S parks on the North American frontier ignited the worldwide conflict known as the French and Indian War in America and the Seven Years' War in Europe. By the conclusion of the war in 1763, fighting had erupted across Europe, North America, the Caribbean, Africa, India and the Philippines. The war in Maine was a parallel war tangentially related to the broader conflict but decidedly local in origin and focus. Likewise, the events leading to renewed war in Maine paralleled the sequence of events precipitating the outbreak of the French and Indian War in Virginia. Subsumed within the greater context of the worldwide conflict, the nearly eighty-year frontier conflict in Maine reached its ultimate conclusion with the English conquest of New France. For the native people of the Northeast, the fall of New France forced them into unilateral dependence on the English and ended the long-standing stratagem of preserving their autonomy by maneuvering between competing European powers. For the English-speaking inhabitants of New England, the collapse of New France removed barriers to expansion and ushered in a wave of explosive population growth and land acquisition along former frontiers.

On the eve of the French and Indian War, New France arched across the North American continent from the Gulf of St. Lawrence to the Gulf of Mexico. This vast territory, composed of the administratively separate colonies of Acadia, Canada and Louisiana, was connected by a nearly contiguous inland waterway originating at the mouth of the St. Lawrence River, extending through the Great Lakes and down the Mississippi River to New Orleans. A network of smaller rivers cutting through the frontiers of America linked this strategically vital water route facilitating trade and diplomacy with native people from Maine and the Maritimes to the Pays de Haute of the Great Lakes and the Midwest.

The expansion of English influence into areas through which many of these tributary rivers flowed, particularly in the Ohio River Valley of western Pennsylvania and Virginia, caused growing concern among governing officials of New France. In 1749, the governor general of Canada, Marquis de la Jonquiere, dispatched a small military force from Montreal to the borderlands of the Ohio to reaffirm French sovereignty over the region's land and native people. Leaving a series of lead markers along the frontier, this band of French soldier-diplomats proclaimed French possession of the region while warning away enterprising English traders.

Emerging from King George's War (War of Austrian Succession) in a position of relative strength, French officials in Paris, like Jonquiere in Canada, expressed renewed interest in the frontiers of North America. In 1752, following Jonquiere's death, Marquis Ange de Menneville Duquesne arrived in Quebec as Canada's new governor general. A more naturally assertive leader than Jonquiere, Duquesne arrived in North America with explicit orders from Paris to secure the vital waterways and frontiers of New France. In the spring of 1753, Duquesne, according to his orders, initiated the construction of a series of forts along the North American frontier.

England's colonial governments, as well as the Crown's Privy Council and Board of Trade, were alarmed by the provocative nature of French activities. On August 28, 1753, the secretary of state for the Southern Department, who was responsible for affairs in America, wrote a letter addressed to the colonial governors advising them of the Crown's intention to resist French expansion in America. In his letter, the Earl of Holderness informed the governors of the Crown's desire

> that you may, at all events, be in a condition to resist any hostile attempts
> that may be made upon any parts of His Majesty's Dominions within your
> Government; and to direct you in the King's Name, that in case the subjects
> of any Foreign Prince or State should presume to make any encroachment
> on the limits of His Majty's dominions, or to erect Forts on His majesty's
> Land, or commit any other act of hostility…you are then to draw forth the
> armed Forces of the province, and to use your best endeavors to repel them
> by force.[135]

Both Lieutenant Governor Robert Dinwiddie of Virginia and Governor William Shirley of Massachusetts seized on this directive, moving toward the use of military force to expel the French from their colonies' hinterlands.

During the fall of 1753, Lieutenant Governor Dinwiddie selected twenty-one-year-old Major George Washington as an envoy to the French commander of the newly constructed Fort LeBoeuf in northwest Pennsylvania. Traversing hundreds of miles of wilderness, Washington delivered a message from Dinwiddie to the fort's commander, Captain Jacques Legardeur de St.-Pierre. Dinwiddie's letter informed the French of Britain's sovereignty over the Ohio Country and requested the French abandon their forts and future aspirations in the region. Legardeur politely rebuffed Washington and Dinwiddie's appeal, indicating his intention of maintaining the newly established French forts as he had been ordered to do by his superiors. Noting apparent French preparations to expand their chain of forts, Washington returned to Williamsburg delivering Legardeur's reply and his observations to Dinwiddie.

Meanwhile, Maine was awash with rumors of French forts and hostile Indian intentions. In late January 1754, Captain William Lithgow of Fort Richmond furnished a report of French efforts to build a fort and establish a settlement at the head of the Kennebec River.[136] Over the next several months, Massachusetts received additional reports from Lithgow and Captain Samuel Goodwin at Frankfort (Dresden) indicating the possibility of renewed native attacks against the Maine communities and the establishment of French forts on the Kennebec River, the Penobscot River and the "Back of Mount Disert Hills."[137] Communiqués from Lithgow indicating French efforts to incite the Canadian mission village Indians to violence and the recent murder of two natives on Matinicus Island heightened concerns about the possible return of hostilities to the region.

Throughout the late winter and spring of 1754, Massachusetts dispatched several officers serving on the Maine frontier—including Captain John North of Fort Frederick at Pemaquid, Lieutenant Thomas Fletcher from St. George's fort and Captain Jonathan Bean (Bane) of the blockhouse at Saco—to locate the supposed French fort and settlement on the Kennebec. All parties returned from their excursions without encountering any evidence of a French presence in Maine. Despite the lack of evidence concerning French encroachments on the lands of King George II, Governor Shirley moved forward with plans to roll back the frontier along the Kennebec. In an address to the General Court on March 28, 1754, Shirley informed the house and council:

William Lithgow had a long and distinguished record as a soldier and officer on the Maine frontier. Having served as the armorer at St. George's fort, Lithgow went on to command Fort Richmond and, later, Fort Halifax. *Colby College Museum of Art. Joseph Badger; Colonel William Lithgow, circa 1760, oil on canvas.*

*I likewise Ordered an Officer, commissioned by me for that Purpose to Proceed by the first Opportunity, to the Suppos'd Place of the New French Settlement, in Order to discover the Certainty & Circumstances of it, & to require the French Commandant to retire and withdraw the People under his Command from that Spot as being under his Majesty's Dominion & within the limits of this Government.*

*And I doubt not, Gentlemen…but that upon a refusal of the French to comply with that Requisition, You will make sufficient Provision for enabling me to Compel them, with the Arm'd Force of the Province, to free it from their Incroachments.*[138]

In the same address to the General Court, Shirley called for the construction of a fort "near the head of the River Kennebec, above the settlements of the Norridgewock Indians."[139] Citing the construction of a French fort recently built on the St. John's River, Shirley goaded the General Court to action, proclaiming:

*A short Delay to dislodge them from their Incroachments near the River Kennebec might give them an Opportunity of making themselves Masters of that River likewise, in the End; And in that Case we may Expect soon to see another Fort Built by them near the Mouth of it and the French in Possession of all the Sea Coast between that and the River St. Johns.*[140]

Based on Governor Shirley's recommendations and the machinations of wealthy, politically connected individuals, the General Court of Massachusetts granted approval for a major military expedition and the construction of a substantial fort to secure the Kennebec from the French.

Neither Shirley nor Dinwiddie possessed the ability to execute the Crown's directive to repel the French by force of arms without the acquiescence of their colonial legislatures. Without promises of Crown subsidies, parsimonious provincial assemblies were typically reluctant to underwrite expensive military undertakings. The Louisbourg expedition had been the exception to this rule. Although the Crown eventually reimbursed Massachusetts for a portion of the expenses incurred, local moneyed interests exerting political influence ultimately made the undertaking possible. As in 1745, Shirley's and Dinwiddie's frontier ventures were enabled and perhaps driven by well-connected financial interests.

The investors of the Ohio Company covetously viewed the lands of trans-Appalachian Virginia and Pennsylvania for their immense economic potential. In 1745, the House of Burgess, Virginia's legislature, granted the land speculation company proprietary rights to three hundred square miles of land at the forks of the Ohio and Monongahela Rivers in the heart of the Ohio Country.[141] Among the names of the wealthy, influential Tidewater families owning interests in the company were Washington and Lee. In 1751, upon his arrival in America as the lieutenant governor of Virginia, the company awarded Robert Dinwiddie one of twenty company shares in hopes of securing the services of the colonies' most powerful individual and closest association to the Crown. Although the cash value of Dinwiddie's stock was substantial, the true value of this asset lay in the 5 percent share of earnings he stood to reap from the development of the company's land.[142] Following King George's War, the company began to exploit its holdings, but French aspirations in the area promised to derail the efforts of the Ohio Company before they came to fruition.

In 1749, the Kennebec Proprietors reinvigorated the claims of the Plymouth Patent along the Kennebec River. Consisting of shareholders from among Boston's political, social and merchant elite, the Kennebec Proprietors, like the Ohio Company, sought to capitalize on the sale and improvement of land within their grant. The vast tract of three million acres claimed by the Kennebec Proprietors had lain fallow since the conclusion of King Philip's War in 1678. Uninhabited by the English at the outbreak of the war, the area was closed to European resettlement in accordance with the Treaty of Casco and all subsequent peace agreements. In 1750, the Kennebec Proprietors sent one of their own, Samuel Goodwin, to begin surveying the company's lands in preparation for future development and serve as the company's agent in Maine. Two years later, the proprietors established the community of Frankfort in present Dresden. For the protection of the town's recently arrived German and French Huguenot inhabitants, the proprietors constructed Fort Frankfort, later renamed Fort Shirley, approximately a mile north of Fort Richmond on the Kennebec River. The new community and fort at Frankfort clearly violated previous understandings concerning the limits of English land rights on the river. Only thirty years before, the native people of the Kennebec had gone to war over the settlements of Cork, Swan Island and Somerset just below the new community at Frankfort. In 1753, Samuel Goodwin and William Lithgow reached an agreement with Norridgewock leaders assuaging their concerns over Frankfort and allowing for limited development of company lands north of Merrymeeting Bay. Unable to further exploit their holdings, the proprietors seized upon the crisis precipitated by rumors of French encroachments on the Kennebec to promote their own interests. Backing Shirley's proposal to expel the French by force and construct a fort in the heart of Norridgewock territory, the powerful members of the Kennebec Proprietors helped push the measure through the General Court.

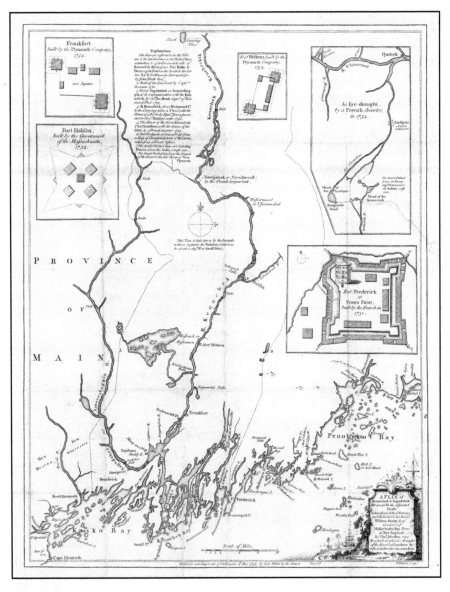

Thomas Johnston map. This is one of two nearly identical maps created for both the Pejeepscot and Kennebec Proprietors for use as evidence in their court wrangling over land title. The map clearly shows the location of the forts along the Kennebec and midcoast, as well as the location of the former Norridgewock village. *Collections of the Maine Historical Society.*

On July 4, 1754, an army of eight hundred men under the command of Major General John Winslow set sail from Falmouth bound for the Kennebec. At the same time, hundreds of miles away in the wilderness of the Ohio Country, Lieutenant Colonel George Washington was surrendering his bedraggled force of several hundred Virginia provincials to the French. In mid-April, Governor Dinwiddie, securing the support of Virginia's legislature, sent Washington and his men to retake the forks of the Ohio at present Pittsburgh from the French. Over the winter, French forces had seized the strategically important confluence of the Ohio and Monongahela Rivers from the Virginians who had established a small outpost there. In late May, while proceeding to the Ohio, Washington surprised and ambushed a detachment of French soldiers on a diplomatic mission to Virginia, resulting in the death of the commanding French officer. Falling back to await reinforcements before proceeding on to the forks, Washington established a small fort, known as Fort Necessity, at Great Meadows in southwest Pennsylvania. On July 3, a mixed force of over six hundred French, Canadians and natives surrounded Fort Necessity, compelling Washington to surrender. In the terms of capitulation, Washington unwittingly admitted to the assassination of Joseph Coulon de Villers de Jumonville, the French officer killed during Washington's earlier ambush. Washington's admission of guilt set in motion a chain of events igniting the fuse of the French and Indian War in America and the Seven Years' War in Europe.

General John Winslow led the Massachusetts expedition to establish Fort Halifax and drive the French from the upper reaches of the Kennebec. Winslow went on to command Massachusetts provincial forces in Acadia and at Lake George. *Collections of the Maine Historical Society.*

As Washington's defeated men marched back to Virginia, Winslow's men made their way up the Kennebec River to expel the French from lands claimed by Massachusetts. After several days at Fort Richmond, the expedition proceeded to the Kennebec's head of navigation in present Augusta. Leading up to the expedition, the Kennebec Proprietors agreed to assist the efforts of Massachusetts by constructing a fort at their own expense "at or near Cushenock, as the Governor shall order,"[143] with the purpose of receiving supplies for the larger and less accessible provincial fort to be constructed farther upriver. In April 1754, the proprietors provided guidelines for the proposed fort, specifying:

> *A house of hewn timber not less than ten inches thick, one hundred feet long, thirty two feet wide and sixteen feet high for the reception of the said Province stores, with conveniences for lodging the soldiers placed there by the government; and will picquet in the same at thirty feet distance from every part of said house, and build a blockhouse of twenty-four feet square at the two opposite angles.*[144]

Over the latter half of July, under the direction of Gershom Flagg, himself a shareholder in the Plymouth Patent, the proprietors erected the fortified storehouse, naming it Fort Western.

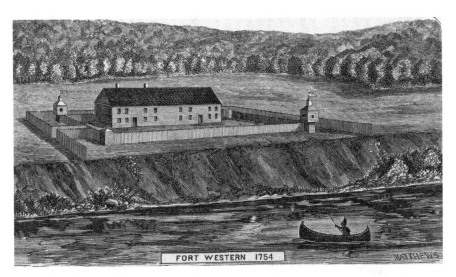

Fort Western. Built and paid for by the Kennebec Proprietors, a group of wealthy and influential land speculators, the fort served as the storehouse for Fort Halifax seventeen miles upriver. *Collections of the Maine Historical Society.*

Fort Western today. It is the oldest surviving wooden fort in North America. Today, it is maintained and operated as a museum by the City of Augusta. *Author's photo.*

As July turned into August, Winslow, along with the main part of his army, ascended the Kennebec River above Fort Western. Following a council of war with his senior officers on July 27, Winslow selected a site for the new provincial fort at Taconnet seventeen miles above Fort Western in what is now the town of Winslow. As construction of the new fort commenced, a force of 500 men traversed the Kennebec River in search of the rumored French fort and settlement. On August 23, having traveled as far as the Chaudière River and the border of Canada, the men of Winslow's army returned, reporting no indications of French activity anywhere along the Kennebec. By the end of the month, General Winslow and most of the men enlisted for the expedition had departed the Kennebec, leaving William Lithgow and the 120 men under his command to garrison the cold, lonely, isolated outpost now known as Fort Halifax.

The greatest beneficiaries of Massachusetts's foray into the Maine wilderness were the Kennebec Proprietors. In 1749 and again in 1753, the proprietors had appealed to the government of Massachusetts for the establishment of a fort at Taconnet to further their corporate ambitions.[145]

Built by the government of Massachusetts in 1754, the construction of Fort Halifax violated previous understandings regarding the limits of English territorial expansion along the Kennebec River and precipitated the final round of war on the Maine frontier. *Detail, collections of the Maine Historical Society.*

Unable to secure the cooperation of government at the time, the proprietors readily seized upon Shirley's proposal in 1754. Within months of rolling back the frontier on the Kennebec, Governor Shirley was awarded a full share in the Plymouth Patent in recognition of his services to the proprietors.[146] Coincidentally, most of the information concerning French encroachments in Maine emanated from Samuel Goodwin and William Lithgow, both of whom were linked to the Kennebec Proprietors. In his March speech before the General Court, which precipitated events in Maine during the summer of 1754, Shirley referenced "accounts sent me from Richmond Fort & Declarations…by two of the Settlers at Frankfort upon River Kennebec."[147] Clearly, the reports from Fort Richmond came from William Lithgow, while Samuel Goodwin was undoubtedly one of the settlers at Frankfort. As a shareholder in the Plymouth Patent and the company's agent on the

Kennebec, Goodwin's ties to the proprietors are unambiguous. Lithgow's ties are more circuitous but just as clear. Lithgow arrived on the Kennebec years before as part of Robert Temple's attempt to establish settlements along the Kennebec prior to Dummer's War. Through his connections to Temple, himself a shareholding member of the Kennebec Proprietors, Lithgow had received land grants and recommendations for promotion in light of his services to the company.[148] Questions will continue to persist about the veracity of and motives behind Goodwin's and Lithgow's reports. However, French designs on the waterways of the North American frontier are incontrovertible. Unlike the exploits of Dinwiddie and Washington, Shirley's military adventure into the wilderness of Maine did not trigger a worldwide conflict. Although Winslow's expedition failed to uncover French encroachments along the Kennebec, it nonetheless plunged the Maine frontier into another spasm of violence.

The native people of Maine and the Canadian mission villages interpreted the establishment of Fort Western and Fort Halifax as clear indications of Massachusetts's hostile and expansionist designs. Not only did the forts violate eighty years of treaty understandings, but the construction of Fort Halifax also severed the Penobscot's primary link with Canada. Located at the confluence of the Sebasticook and Kennebec Rivers, Fort Halifax was located only fifty miles from the Penobscot and situated along the Penobscot people's principal canoe route to the Kennebec and Canada. Although Governor Shirley conferred with and offered gifts to representatives of both the Penobscot and Norridgewock over the summer of 1754, more militant factions of Maine native people were not placated by Massachusetts's presents and platitudes of peace. In November 1754, just months after the establishment of the outpost, a party of mission village Indians descended on Fort Halifax, killing and scalping one soldier and taking four others captive.

With the clouds of war building over Maine, conciliatory resident Penobscot sought to preserve peaceful relations with Massachusetts over the winter of 1755. In February, Lieutenant Thomas Fletcher of the St. George garrison wrote to Governor Shirley, informing him:

> *I have Received advise from the Chefs of the Penobscot Tribe and tho' proper to inform Your Excellency They told me that in the Spring there would be a great number of Canada Indians at their Village; I asked them what they thot their business was they said they could not tell but they thot to do mischief…for that the French for years past had done all they could to break the Peace that now Subsists between your Excelency And us a few days ago*

*the French sent us A hatchet urged us to take it and strike the English We*
*told them we should not whilst the Kings were at peace and they were angry*
*and threatened us.*[149]

During the next several months, the Penobscot continued to provide Massachusetts with intelligence. In early May, based on information obtained from the Penobscot, Lieutenant Fletcher advised Captain Lithgow at Fort Halifax "that a Body of the Noridgwalk and Assaguntoocook Indians are Going A Gainst The people On the Kennebec River."[150]

Within days of Fletcher's warning, attacks resumed against Fort Halifax and the exposed eastern communities. Throughout May and early June, the midcoast was rocked by a series of raids conducted against St. George (Thomaston, Warren and Cushing), Broad Bay (Waldoboro), Pleasant Point (Cushing), Sheepscot (Newcastle),[151] Frankfort (Dresden) and North Yarmouth (Yarmouth, Freeport and Harpswell). Outside the walls of Fort Halifax, one soldier was shot and killed while another was taken captive. Farther to the west, additional attacks were carried out against the settlements of Gorham and New Glouster.

Massachusetts responded to the spate of raids by declaring war against all the eastern tribes, exclusive of the Penobscot, on June 10, 1755. In accordance with Dummer's Treaty and the Treaty of Falmouth, Massachusetts called for Penobscot support in the war against their native brethren while pledging material support for their "Invalids, Women and Children, if they will come amongst us and put themselves under our Protection."[152] Submission to the demands of Massachusetts presented the Penobscot with the same dilemma they had faced when called upon to fulfill their treaty obligations at the beginning of King George's War a decade earlier. By choosing to live among the English, the Penobscot would effectively surrender the last remnants of their sovereignty and autonomy to Massachusetts. They also realized the dynamic of cohabitation with the English would prove unsustainable. In a letter to the government, several of the Penobscot's principal leaders expressed their concern of living among the English, stating, "Some of our Young men are rogueish; and our Dogs are not under command and may destroy some of the English's Creatures which would breed bad blood."[153] With these considerations in mind, the Penobscot, as they had during King George's War, remained noncommittal while expressing peaceful intentions and pursuing, to the best of their ability, a policy of passive neutrality.

With the declaration of war, Massachusetts strengthened the garrisons of the region's forts and authorized the establishment of a "marching army" consisting of three hundred men to patrol and protect the communities of the eastern frontier. As had become customary, bounties were established for the taking of native scalps and captives. To promote the services of "volunteers"—quasi-military bands operating outside of government pay, command and control—Massachusetts promised bounty payments exceeding those offered to men serving as provincial soldiers. In June 1755, Governor Shirley offered volunteers £110 for every native captive seized and £100 for every scalp taken regardless of the victim's age or gender.[154] Composed of local inhabitants, the behavior of the volunteer companies reflects many of the prevailing attitudes of the region's predominantly Scots-Irish populace. Prosecuting the war on their own terms and loath to discriminate between hostile and non-hostile natives, the actions of civilian volunteers would undermine prospects for peace over the summer of 1755.

In early July 1755, twenty volunteers under the command of James Cargill left Newcastle in search of scalps. Marching eastward, Cargill picked up an additional eleven volunteers from Broad Bay and St. George. About six miles south of St. George's fort, Cargill and his company crossed the St. George River, entering the homelands of the Penobscot. In present South Thomaston, Cargill's volunteers fell upon a Penobscot family band. After killing and scalping Margaret Moxa (a well-known and respected Penobscot woman), her infant child and husband, the company of volunteers continued their march eastward. Near sunset, the scalp hunters encountered another band of Penobscot on the shores of Owls Head. Opening fire on the unsuspecting natives, Cargill's men killed another nine people, sending the remainder of the native party scrambling for their lives and the cover of the forest. The next day, the volunteers appeared at St. George's fort with the plunder they had obtained during the attacks and the twelve scalps they had cut from the bodies of the dead. Intending to continue his pursuit of the native people, Cargill requested provisions from Captain Bradbury. Infuriated by Cargill's disregard for Massachusetts's peace with the Penobscot, Bradbury refused Cargill's request. Frustrated by Bradbury's lack of cooperation, Cargill dismissed his men, telling "them to Shift Every man for himself" and to "set out for home."[155] Bradbury subsequently lodged a formal complaint against Cargill, leading to his arrest for the murders of Margaret Moxa and eleven other native people. In 1757, Cargill was found not guilty by a jury of his peers and subsequently awarded payment for the scalps he and his men had taken.

Cargill's attacks were not the only instance of frontier lawlessness confronting Bradbury during the early summer of 1755. Just days before

Cargill's murders, Bradbury faced an armed insurrection among his own garrison and the inhabitants of St. George. At the end of June, Bradbury held a conference with nine principal leaders of the Penobscot to discuss their obligations under the Treaty of Falmouth and Massachusetts's desire for continued peace. As the members of the delegation prepared to leave the fort for consultations with their people, they were seized by members of the community and garrison "all in arms & determined that the Indians Should never go of until they had given them Satisfaction."[156] Bradbury, "not being able to use force, thought it best to give Soft words"[157] to resolve the pending crisis. Acknowledging the concerns of the armed mob, Bradbury managed to facilitate a compromise in which several of the Penobscot were held as hostages and sent to Boston while the others were released to confer with their people. Although the incident ended without violence, it helped erode prospects for sustained peace between Massachusetts and the Penobscot.

Over the summer of 1755, Massachusetts attempted to repair the growing rift with the Penobscot. In a series of good faith gestures, Massachusetts released the hostages taken at St. George, distributed gifts to the families of Cargill's victims and promised to bring the perpetrators of the attacks to justice. To prevent further incidents of unprovoked attacks, Massachusetts prohibited provincial and volunteer forces from operating offensively within thirty miles to the east of St. George's fort or within twenty miles of the Penobscot River.[158] Despite the demonstrations of goodwill and attempts to rectify the situation on the eastern frontier, the Penobscot remained aloof to repeated Massachusetts requests to uphold their treaty obligations. In late September, the community at St. George was attacked again by a native war party. Suspecting Penobscot participation in the attack, Massachusetts stepped up pressure on the Penobscot to provide able-bodied men to serve as provincial soldiers and remove themselves from their homelands to the protective umbrella of the white settlements. Increasing frustration over their refusal to submit to the provisions of the Treaty of Falmouth led Massachusetts to declare war against the Penobscot on November 1, 1755.

War, total and complete, returned to the Maine coast with Massachusetts's declaration of war against the Penobscot. The phenomenon was nothing new; war had been a recurrent state of affairs for the past eighty years. The distinction between civilian and military targets, combatants and noncombatants was erased with the initial outbreak of hostilities in 1675. Although the nature of war on the Maine frontier remained unchanged, the language used by Massachusetts in sanctioning its conduct had evolved. By the time of Massachusetts's final declaration of war against the Penobscot

By His HONOUR

# SPENCER PHIPS, Esq;

Lieutenant-Governour and Commander in Chief, in and over His Majesty's Province of the *Massachusetts-Bay* in *New-England.*

# A PROCLAMATION.

WHEREAS the Tribe of *Penobscot* Indians have repeatedly in a perfidious Manner acted contrary to their solemn Submission unto His Majesty long since made and frequently renewed ;

I have therefore, at the Desire of the House of Representatives, with the Advice of His Majesty's Council, thought fit to issue this Proclamation, and to declare the Penobscot Tribe of Indians to be Enemies, Rebels and Traitors to His Majesty King GEORGE the Second : And I do hereby require His Majesty's Subjects of this Province to embrace all Opportunities of pursuing, captivating, killing and destroying all and every of the aforesaid Indians,

*AND WHEREAS* the General Court of this Province have voted that a Bounty or Incouragement be granted and allowed to be paid out of the Publick Treasury, to the marching Forces that shall have been employed for the Defence of the *Eastern* and *Western* Frontiers, from the *First* to the *Twenty-fifth* of this Instant *November* ;

I have thought fit to publish the same ; and I do hereby Promise, That there shall be paid out of the Province-Treasury to all and any of the said Forces, over and above their Bounty upon Inlistment, their Wages and Subsistence, the Premiums or Bounty following, viz.

For every Male *Penobscot* Indian above the Age of Twelve Years, that shall be taken within the Time aforesaid and brought to *Boston, Fifty Pounds.*

For every Scalp of a Male *Penobscot* Indian above the Age aforesaid, brought in as Evidence of their being killed as aforesaid, *Forty Pounds.*

For every Female *Penobscot* Indian taken and brought in as aforesaid, and for every Male Indian Prisoner under the Age of Twelve Years, taken and brought in as aforesaid, *Twenty-five Pounds.*

For every Scalp of such Female Indian or Male Indian under the Age of Twelve Years, that shall be killed and brought in as Evidence of their being killed as aforesaid, *Twenty Pounds.*

Given at the Council-Chamber in *Boston,* this Third Day of *November* 1 7 5 5, and in the Twenty-ninth Year of the Reign of our Sovereign Lord *GEORGE* the Second, by the Grace of GOD of *Great-Britain, France* and *Ireland,* KING, Defender of the Faith, &c.

*By His Honour's Command,*

**J. Willard,** Secr.

**S. Phips.**

## GOD Save the KING.

*BOSTON*: Printed by *John Draper,* Printer to His Honour the Lieutenant-Governour and Council. *1755.*

Spencer Phips's proclamation of war against the Penobscot, 1755. Scalp and captive bounties had been a staple of frontier warfare in Maine since the outbreak of hostilities in the seventeenth century. The significance of this document is not in the pronouncement of the scalp and captive bounties but in the use of language advocating what we would today call genocide: "I do hereby require his Majesty's Subjects of this Province to embrace all Opportunities of pursuing, captivating, killing and destroying all and every of the aforesaid Indians." *Collections of the Massachusetts Historical Society.*

in 1755, the language used to promote its execution resounded with tones of what would today be termed genocide. Acting as the province's chief executive in the absence of Governor William Shirley, Lieutenant Governor Spencer Phips proclaimed, "I do hereby require his Majesty's Subjects of this province to Embrace all opportunities of pursuing, captivating, killing and destroying all and every of the aforesaid Indians."[159]

Native attacks against the eastern communities commenced again in the spring of 1756. Along the St. George River from Pleasant Point in Cushing to what is now Thomaston, no fewer than eight attacks were carried out against fortified garrisons and exposed work parties. In early May, a native war party descending the Androscoggin River committed a series of attacks from the New Meadows River to Flying Point in what is now Freeport. Other attacks occurred outside the palisades of Fort Halifax and the garrison at Arrowsic. Pervasive fear gripped the eastern communities in the aftermath of these raids. Most of the region's inhabitants retreated from their homes to the safety of nearby garrisons. Reports of small native parties lurking about the communities and requests for additional soldiers to protect the garrisons flooded the government of Massachusetts over the spring of 1756. Massachusetts responded to the inhabitants' fears by dispatching soldiers under government pay to the isolated communities and launching a long-range scout up the Androscoggin River to prevent any further attacks coming from Canada along that undefended thoroughfare.

Perhaps more so than the white inhabitants of the eastern communities, the resident native population of Maine suffered tremendously under the weight of war. Hardship, hunger and disease characterized their experience over the course of 1756 and 1757. The activities of Massachusetts provincial scouts and civilian volunteers caused serious disruptions to the seasonal subsistence patterns of the eastern tribes. Using whaleboats and schooners, volunteer scalp hunters ranged the Maine coast between the St. George River and Mount Desert Island. Although few scalps were taken,[160] the activities of the volunteers and the threat they posed kept the Penobscot people from safely engaging in their traditional harvest of seafood, waterfowl and other shoreline resources. Over the winter of 1757, Massachusetts authorized the establishment of a 150-man scouting expedition to range the upper reaches of the Kennebec, Androscoggin and Saco Rivers to disrupt the traditional winter hunting grounds of the native people calling those river basins home. Along with hunger, smallpox broke out among the Penobscot during the summer and fall of 1756, devastating an already weakened, desperate people. Based on reports from Jabez

Bradbury at St. George, perhaps two-thirds of the Penobscot population perished as a result of the epidemic.[161]

Weary of war, and in need of sustenance, the eastern tribes began making appeals for peace and trade over the winter of 1757. On February 22, 1757, two delegates claiming to represent the Penobscot approached Captain Bradbury at St. George, hoping to begin negotiations with Massachusetts. In the statement they prepared for Lieutenant Governor Phips, the Penobscot indicated, "Our desire is to live in love as formerly we used to do, for what is the reason we should not want that which is good, for it was not we that were the occasion of any breaking of Friendship formerly...The old men in Penobscutt Salute the Governor in Boston."[162]

In a subsequent letter to Bradbury, Phips responded to the Penobscot's plea: "I do not see how it is possible in the present Situation of our own Affairs to permit the Indians to come in & Trade with us as usual: if they would come and live amongst us during the continuance of the War, it is probable the Court would make Some Provision for their Support."[163]

On May 2, in anticipation of the Penobscot representative return to St. George, the General Court informed Bradbury of their agreement with Phips's position. The General Court additionally advised Bradbury: "You must warn them of the Danger they are exposed to by coming in as they do, for our Scouts may possibly meet w[th] them and not discover their Flag of Truce & so do them a mischief."[164]

On May 16, 1757, fourteen representatives of the Penobscot and St. John's people retuned to St. George to receive Massachusetts's answer to their February peace proposal. Conferring with the native delegation, Bradbury delivered Massachusetts's expectations for the resumption of trade and peace while warning them of the dangers inherent in returning to the fort for further discussion. Pressing Bradbury for trade to no avail, the native leaders requested Bradbury relay their continued desire for peace to the government of Massachusetts. Unable to secure either peace or trade, the Penobscot and St. John's delegates dejectedly departed St. George.

While English and native leaders engaged in fruitless discussions over the terms of official peace and trade, a group of natives and individuals from the community dealt in their own illicit trade. Having swapped furs for rum, the exchange turned sour when one of the natives was seized by the local inhabitants looking to cash in on the captive bounty offered by the government. Bringing their prize to the fort, the captors only reluctantly relinquished their claim through the intervention of Joshua Freeman, who commanded the local scouting company. Shortly thereafter, Neptune, one of the chief Penobscot sagamores, entered the fort under a flag of truce to retrieve his brethren. Enraged and rebuffed in his demands for compensatory trade, Neptune defiantly destroyed his flag of truce, declaring there was a sizable body of Canadian Indians at Penobscot ready to wreak vengeance on the English communities. Within hours of Neptune's departure, reports filtered in from local inhabitants indicating Neptune had boasted of being in the presence of twenty-six Indians, expecting to rendezvous with a larger native party also bound for St. George.

In light of recent developments and Neptune's hostile behavior, those at St. George feared the Penobscot's and St. John's previous requests for peace and trade had turned into war cries. To protect the community, Captains Bradbury and Freeman determined to send out a party of scouts the next morning. Unbeknownst to either of the provincial military commanders, a group of volunteers set off in pursuit of the native party that evening. About a mile east of St. George's fort, the volunteers encountered a group of sleeping natives. Musket shots rang out in the darkness, precipitating a short firefight. When the smoke cleared, the volunteers found they had killed one of the natives and stripped him of his scalp.

Within days of the incident at St. George, attacks resumed against the communities of the midcoast. Exposed settlers and work parties were attacked at Matinicus, Broad Bay, Pemaquid, Topsham and New Meadows, while on the Kennebec, natives along the riverbank exchanged musket fire with boat parties hauling supplies between Fort Western and Fort Halifax. Exhausted by war and facing continued threats from volunteers operating from schooners and whaleboats, the native people residing along Penobscot Bay withdrew from their traditional summer habitations, seeking security in remote enclaves and among the St. John's Indians to the east. By mid-June, the raids against the eastern communities had ceased, ushering in a period of quiet vigilance along the Maine frontier.

Fear and desperation plagued the communities of the midcoast throughout the remainder of 1757 and into 1758. More than two years of war and garrison life hampered the inhabitants' ability to tend crops and produce timber products for export. Exacerbating the region's already dire circumstances, an unusually long winter followed by a spring drought resulted in poor crop yields during the 1757 harvest. Broad Bay's petition to the General Court requesting aid and relief summarizes the plight of the eastern communities:

*The Continuation of the Warre, and the cruelty of the Indian Enemy Used here, has been a terror to us and been a Great hinderance to our Labour; Tho* *we bare all that with patience, as long as we were Capable to mentain in some measure, our large Famelys, but now with Tears in our Eyes, must Acquaint Your Hon$^{rs}$ that our harvest is so miserable, as ever been Known by Man Kind,...We therefore hope Your Hon$^{rs}$ will be pleased to take our deplorable case in to Consideration, what Damage it would accrue to the Eastern parts, in case such a Number of Famelys should be forced to breake up, as we are at the borders of the Enemy. Certainly the rest of the Settlements betwixt this, and North Yarmouth would be Obliged to follow Us.[165]*

In March 1758, influential members of the Kennebec Proprietors echoed the concerns of Broad Bay's inhabitants. Appealing to the General Court, the proprietors warned of the collapse of the entire Maine frontier without the "paternal care" of the government following the anticipated resumption of raids in April and May.[166]

Fortunately for the eastern communities and the English-speaking settlements of Maine in general, the expected wave of springtime raids never materialized. Only two attacks were conducted against the midcoast during the planting season. The first attack occurred at Meduncook (Friendship) in late May when the Bradford family became victims of native raiders. The second raid came in early June when the Preble family was attacked in what is today Woolwich and the Pomeroy family in Frankfort (Dresden) was taken captive. The exhaustion of Maine's resident native population and developments in the war beyond the borders of Maine likely contributed to the decline in attacks against the region's coastal communities. Despite several years of success in their war against the British in North America, the French feared for the very survival of New France by 1758. Concerned with preserving Canada, the French could ill afford to support the interests of its native allies along the frontiers of North America. British and provincial efforts over the summer and early autumn effectively severed the spine of New France. The destruction of Fort Frontenac on the shores of Lake Ontario by General John Bradstreet and the seizure of Fort Duquesne at the forks of the Ohio broke the chain of waterways connecting the western portions of New France. In the east, the British retook Louisbourg, cutting off Canada's access to France through the Gulf of St. Lawrence. In New Brunswick, the British fervently and brutally routed out the remnants of Micmac and Acadian resistance to British domination of the Canadian Maritimes.

Although the midcoast was spared the usual spate of attacks during May and June 1758, the largest attack against the Maine frontier during the entire war was delivered in late August. In mid-August, Governor

Charles Deschamps de Boishebert. Holding a commission in the Compagnie Franches de la Marine, the provincial military establishment of New France, Boishebert earned the reputation of a formidable partisan fighter with the Acadians of Nova Scotia and New Brunswick. Boishebert led the 1758 expedition that attacked St. George's fort (Thomaston) and the surrounding area. *Courtesy of Wikimedia Commons.*

Thomas Pownall, who succeeded William Shirley as the royal governor of Massachusetts in 1757, received intelligence about the impending attack from Lieutenant Colonel Robert Moncton, who was leading British efforts to crush Acadian resistance in New Brunswick. According to Moncton, a mixed force of French Acadians and Indians under the command of Charles Deschamps de Boishebert had departed Miramichi bound for the coast of Maine.[167] Embarking troops and supplies from Castle William in Boston Harbor aboard the province man-of-war *King George* and the armed province sloop *Massachusetts*, Pownall set sail for the St. George River. After supplementing the garrison and supplies at St. George's fort, the *King George* and the *Massachusetts* reconnoitered in Penobscot Bay searching for the enemy. Just west of Mount Desert Island, the two Massachusetts vessels encountered Boishebert's expedition. Due to unfavorable winds, the *King George* and the *Massachusetts*, both square-rigged vessels with limited ability to sail into the wind, became wind bound, while the French and Indian flotilla of bateaux and canoes slipped down the bay for St. George. For several days at the end of August 1758, Boishebert's force of approximately 250 French and Indians laid siege to St. George's fort while destroying property and killing cattle across the community. The siege was broken when the *Massachusetts*, gaining a favorable wind and tide, finally made its way up the St. George River to relieve the fort. Realizing they would be unable to take the fort, the French and Indians abandoned their siege of St. George and struck at nearby Meduncook (Friendship) and Broad Bay (Waldoboro). At Meduncook, they killed and captured 8 people while at nearby Broadbay they attacked the settlement's garrisons, plundered abandoned homes and destroyed crops and livestock.

By January 1759, Governor Pownall was committed to pushing the Maine frontier eastward from St. George to the head of Penobscot Bay. Proposals had been offered to this effect before. Governor Shirley advocated for the same measure toward the end of King George's War in 1748 and again in 1756. Massachusetts had been financially, militarily and politically unable and unwilling to act upon Shirley's previous recommendations. However, the weakening of the eastern tribes and the looming collapse of French Canada portended a new era of military and political considerations. In January 1758, Governor Pownall wrote to Prime Minister William Pitt seeking British support for his plan to establish a fort on Penobscot Bay. Having secured political and financial backing for the enterprise from both Prime Minister Pitt and Jeffery Amherst, the commander in chief of British force in North America, Pownall addressed the General Court of Massachusetts in February 1759

Thomas Pownall replaced William Shirley as the royal governor of Massachusetts. Pownall led the expedition to establish a fort and trading post bearing his name at the mouth of the Penobscot River, seizing Penobscot lands by "right of conquest." *Courtesy of Lincoln County Historical Association.*

asking for authorization to bring his plans to fruition. Granting approval for the establishment of the new fort, Massachusetts moved forward to launch a military expedition into the heart of Penobscot territory over the spring of 1759.

In early May, Pownall traveled to Falmouth to assume command of the expedition bound for Penobscot. A provincial army of four hundred men from Maine was raised and equipped to spearhead the seizure of the Penobscot's territory. To facilitate the speedy construction of the new outpost, components of the fort were prefabricated at Falmouth under the direction of Gershom Flagg, who had been responsible for the erection of Fort Western in 1754. On May 8, the expedition, led by Governor Pownall and his second in command, Samuel Waldo,[168] embarked upon transports and set sail for St. George. After several days at St. George, the expedition proceeded on to the head of Penobscot Bay and the mouth of the Penobscot River. Landing at present Cape Jellison in Stockton Springs, soldiers of the expedition ranged the lands adjacent to the river to root out possible Penobscot resistance and scout the area for a suitable site for the new fort. Near the falls in present Brewer, Samuel Waldo, who accompanied the scouts, dropped dead, ending his proprietary and entrepreneurial aspirations in Maine. After surveying the river, it was decided to begin construction of newly named Fort Pownall on a point of land not far from the original landing site. By July 6, 1759, the fort was completed, marking the symbolic end to the wars that had devastated the coast of Maine.

While at St. George in early May, Pownall had conferred with a series of Penobscot and St. John's representatives seeking peace and trade. When

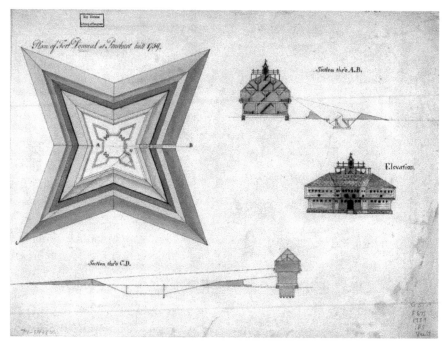

Plan of Fort Pownall. Built in 1759, the presence of the fort moved the frontier of Maine from the midcoast to the head of Penobscot Bay. Located at the mouth of the Penobscot River, the fort closed off the native people's last available waterway to the Atlantic. *Courtesy of the Library of Congress.*

Pownall departed St. George on May 13 bound for Penobscot, he brought with him four of the native delegates who had approached him to conduct negotiations. Upon landing his army in the heart of Penobscot territory, Pownall dispatched these native leaders with gifts of rum, meat, shot, powder, blankets, shoes, caps, a gun, a flag of truce and a message to their people. In his message to the native people, Pownall stated:

> *I am come to build a fort at Penobscot, and will make the land English. I am able to do it—and I will do it. If they say I shall not, let them come and Defend their land now in this time of War...As to the People of Penobscot, I seek not their Favour nor fear them, for they can do me neither good nor harm. I am sorry for their Distress, and would do them Good. Let them become English, they and their Wives and Families, and come and live under the Protection of the Fort.*[169]

The message was clear: the eastern tribes were a defeated people. Although the Penobscot offered no resistance to the seizure of their homelands, Massachusetts remained steadfast in its expectation that they uphold the expectations of Dummer's Treaty and the Treaty of Falmouth.

Fort Pownall not only stood in the epicenter of the Penobscot's homelands, but its location at the mouth of the Penobscot River also closed off the native people's last water route access to the coast and the Gulf of Maine. Events in Canada over the remainder of 1759 and 1760 struck further blows to the region's native people. In October 1759, the mission village at St. Francis was attacked and destroyed by British forces under the command of Robert Rogers, scattering, shattering and demoralizing many of those native people who had previously fled Maine. The fall of Quebec in September 1759 was followed a year later by the capture of Montreal and the conquest of French Canada by the British. Unable to obtain trade goods or military support from the French, Maine's native people could no longer play the middle ground between competing European powers. With little or no political cohesion, the people of the eastern tribes found themselves politically and militarily impotent.

Although no further native attacks were conducted against the settlements following the establishment of Fort Pownall, the absence of bloodshed did not necessarily mean peace had returned to the region. No formal treaty concluded the final war between Massachusetts and the eastern tribes. Tensions over trade and land continued to strain relations between the native people and the ever-growing number of white settlers on the Maine frontier. Sporadic threats of violence continued to plague Maine in the wake of repeated murders and abuses of native people at the hands of their white neighbors. Unable to effectively negotiate on their own behalf or forcefully promote their interests, the Penobscot finally declared their submission to Massachusetts in a 1769 address to Governor Francis Bernard in which they proclaimed: "We acknowledge that we have sided with your Enemies and that they and we have been conquered, and that we are become the subjects of that great King George. We do now in the name of our whole Tribe recognize it, and do declare that we are now and always will be, ready to obey his call upon any duty whatever."[170]

In scattered family bands, Maine's native people continued to live quietly in the forests and along the waterways of their former homelands. As shadows of their former selves, the native people of Maine faded from the forefront of history. So, too, did the memory of the long, bitter struggle between opposing cultures who sought to call Maine home.

# Notes

## CHAPTER 1

1. The dates given reflect the dates as they pertain to the conflicts in Maine. In several instances, King William's War and King George's War in particular, the conflict in Maine dragged on for longer than is traditionally recognized elsewhere. In the case of the French and Indian War, the conflict in Maine ended in 1759 for all intents and purposes, but the Treaty of Paris, which formally concluded hostilities between the warring European factions, was not signed until 1763.
2. Haefeli and Sweeney, *Captors and Captives*.
3. Brack, *Norumbega Reconsidered*, 83.
4. Harold Prins, "Turmoil on the Wabanaki Frontier," in Judd, Churchill and Eastman, *Maine*, 108.
5. Cronon, *Changes in the Land*, 83.
6. Bourque, *Twelve Thousand Years*. Bourque offers an interpretation of indigenous ethno-history based largely on French sources such as Champlain, Baird and Lescarbot. Bourque's interpretation is currently the most widely subscribed to school of thought pertaining to the Native Americans of Maine. There is a countervailing argument to Bourque's position offered by H.G. Brack of the Davistown Museum in his book *Norumbega Reconsidered*. Brack asserts that the residents of

the midcoast region were more ethnically aligned with the eastern Abenaki than the Echtemin.

7. Many spellings were used to denote the native people living along the Androscoggin River. For the sake of consistency, I have adopted the spelling "Amarascoggin" throughout the text.

8. In period texts, the term "Tarrentine" seems to refer collectively to the Penobscot, St. John and Cape Sable tribes. There are references to Canibas Indians moving to the Penobscot region, and it seems likely that there was some intermixing of ethnic groups as a result of the upheavals caused by the great pandemic and the intertribal warfare of the early seventeenth century

9. "Submission and Agreements of the Eastern Indians," in *Documentary History of the State of Maine*, vol. X, Maine Historical Society, ed. James Phinney Baxter, 10–11.

10. David L. Ghere, "Diplomacy and War on the Maine Frontier," in *Maine*, ed. Judd, Churchill and Eastman, 108.

11. Williamson, *History of the State of Maine*, 516; Leamon, *Revolution Downeast*, 6. Leamon estimates that the population of Maine stood at two thousand during King William's War and twelve thousand in 1743. He claims that twenty years later in 1763, the population had reached about twenty-three thousand.

# CHAPTER 2

12. In 1675, Swansea was part of the Plymouth Colony and not part of the Massachusetts Bay Colony.

13. When considered from the perspective of total population, the losses of King Philip's War far surpass those of any other war in American history. When the losses of the indigenous population are figured into this equation, the magnitude of the war is truly staggering. English losses alone based on per capita figures are seven times greater than those of World War II and double the losses of the Civil War. Native losses are estimated to be tenfold that of the English. Shultz and Tougais, *King Philip's War*, 4–5.

14. Wheeler and Wheeler, *History of Brunswick*, 788–97. The location of Purchase's house is the subject of confusion. Some records assert that he resided at the head of the New Meadows River, while others believe that his dwelling was located at Fish House Hill in Brunswick. It is known that Purchase was involved in the trade of salmon, which Wheeler believes gives credence to his habitation being near the falls and Fish House Hill.

15. Shultz and Tougias, *King Philip's War*, 304.
16. During this period and until 1752, both the Julian and Gregorian calendars were in use. The Julian calendar recognized the New Year as beginning in March, while the Gregorian calendar used January to mark the beginning of the New Year. During the time in which both calendars were in use, the contested months of January and February were denoted with the use of both years and expressed as 1675/76, for example.
17. Greene, *History of Boothbay*, 88.
18. Ibid., 89.
19. Williamson, *History of the State of Maine*, 545.
20. Ibid., 552–53.
21. Johnston, *History of the Towns of Bristol and Breman*, 171.
22. Ibid.
23. Drake, *Border Wars of New England*, 49–50.
24. Williamson, *History of the State of Maine*, 625.
25. Parkman, *Frontenac and New France*, 247.
26. Ibid., 258.
27. Drake, *Border Wars of New England*, 73.
28. Bradley and Camp, *Forts of Pemaquid*, 10.
29. Ibid., 36–51.
30. Maine Historical Society, *Documentary History of Maine*, vol. 10, 8.

# CHAPTER 3

31. Williamson, *History of the State of Maine*, vol. II, 37. Williamson estimates the population of Maine as being between five and six thousand in 1702. This would put Maine's losses at between 11 and 12 percent.
32. Ibid., vol. 1, 650.
33. John G. Reid, "Political Definitions: Creating Maine and Acadia," in *American Beginnings*, ed. Baker, et al, 176.
34. Haefeli and Sweeny, *Captive Histories*, 5.
35. Lozier, "In Each Other's Arms."
36. New France experienced chronic labor shortages throughout the period, and the dearth of available labor was exacerbated during times of war when the influx of new labor was curtailed and the existing labor pool was drained by military obligations.
37. Acts and Resolves…, vol. 1, 175.

38. Ibid., 176.
39. Bourque, *Twelve Thousand Years*, 175.
40. Divergent views of the proceedings exist between two of the attendees. Judge Samuel Penhallow wrote of the Penobscot's unambiguous declaration of peaceful desires and intentions, while Father Sebastian Rale, who accompanied the delegation from Norridgewock, described their assertion that the natives shared a brotherhood based on religion and that if the English took up the hatchet against the French, their native brothers would fight alongside the French. These differing views may be attributed to several possible explanations. Perhaps the Penobscot and Norridgewock held widely divergent political outlooks. It may also speak to the fundamental misunderstanding between the two cultures and faulty translation and perception. It may also reflect the Norridgewock telling Father Rale, their resident missionary, something different than they told the English, or it may have been a case of Rale's own self-serving record of the proceedings.
41. Calvert, *Black Robe on the Kennebec*, 143.
42. Williamson, *History of the State of Maine*, vol. II, 46.
43. Ibid.
44. It was unclear at the time what had happened to the inhabitants of Norridgewock and why it was abandoned. It was later revealed through a letter written by the Jesuit missionary Sebastian Rale that the inhabitants of the village had learned of Hilton's expedition and had fled to the mission village of St. Francis.
45. Williamson, *History of the State of Maine*, vol. II, 64.
46. Bourque, *Twelve Thousand Years*, 180.
47. Ibid.
48. Calvert, *Black Robe on the Kennebec*, 161.
49. Williamson, *History of the State of Maine*, vol. II, 68.
50. Ibid.

# CHAPTER 4

51. "Submission and Agreements of the Eastern Indians," in Maine Historical Society, *Documentary History of the State of Maine*, vol. XXIII, ed. James Phinney Baxter, 85.
52. Gyles was taken captive as a young boy during the 1689 attack against Fort Charles and the community at Pemaquid. After living among the

Penobscot/St. John people for several years, Gyles was sold to a French trader who, in turn, ransomed him back to the English. Due to his familiarity with the native language as a result of his captivity, Gyles went on to serve as an interpreter as well as military official on the Maine coast throughout the early eighteenth century. John Gyles recorded his experiences as a captive in his 1736 *Memoirs of Odd Adventures.*

53. The exact date of Fort Richmond's construction is unclear. Certainly it was established no later than 1722, and likely it had been built somewhat earlier. For more information regarding Fort Richmond and the earlier garrisons, see Reverend Henry O'Thayer, *Fort Richmond, Maine,* in Collections of the Maine Historical Society, Second Series, vol. 5, 129–60.

54. Plummer, *History of Bath,* 57.

55. Ibid., 58.

56. Eaton, *History of Thomaston,* 31.

57. There are several possible interpretations to this statement. One explanation is that Madockawando had fled from either the Kennebec or St. John's to the Penobscot as an orphan in the wake of an epidemic during the mid-1600s. Although Madockawando was not a Penobscot by birth, he was, for whatever reason, quickly adopted by and recognized as a leader among their people (see Bourque, *Twelve Thousand Years*). Another possibility is that the native people who voiced their objections to the agents of the Muscongus Patent were not themselves Penobscot but local Wawenock who traditionally resided in the area between the Sheepscot and St. George Rivers. By the late seventeenth century, the Wawenock seem to have largely disappeared from the historic record, although representatives identified as Wawenock participated in the negotiations of the seventeenth century. It seems apparent that many of the Wawenock migrated to the French mission village at Becancour and those who remained became clients of the more powerful Penobscot to their east. A final explanation may be found in the native people's belief that one generation could not speak for subsequent generations and that Madockawando's death in 1698 and the subsequent passage of time negated arrangements he had made for his people in his lifetime.

58. "Submission and Agreements of the Eastern Indians," in Maine Historical Society, *Documentary History of the State of Maine,* vol. XXIII, ed. James Phinney Baxter, 107–8.

59. Williamson, *History of the State of Maine,* vol. II, 106.

60. Ibid., 106–7.

61. Acts and Resolves…, vol. II, 258.

62. Ibid., vol. X, 216.

63. Ibid., 218.

64. "Submission and Agreements of the Eastern Indians," in Maine Historical Society, *Documentary History of the State of Maine*, vol. X, ed. James Phinney Baxter, 146.

65. Eaton, *History of Thomaston*, 34.

66. Allied natives served with the English throughout the wars that ravaged the coast. The full story is beyond the scope of this work, but interestingly, they were often employed in the use of whaleboats, with which they had developed considerable proficiency due to their work as whalers in the surf whaling industry that flourished off Cape Cod and Rhode Island.

67. Williamson, *History of the State of Maine*, vol. II, 127.

68. Ibid. This was not the first time that the native people had used captured vessels in their conduct of war with the English. In fact, the use of European vessels by native people can be traced back to at least the early seventeenth century with the use of European-obtained shallops by the Micmac people. Although they seemingly used captive boat crews to some extent, the native people were not wholly bereft of sailing skills themselves.

69. "Submission and Agreements of the Eastern Indians," in Maine Historical Society, *Documentary History of the State of Maine*, vol. XXIII, ed. Baxter, 166.

70. Penhallow, *History of the Wars of New England*, 103, n. 29.

71. Calvert, *Black Robe on the Kennebec*, 197.

72. Ibid., 201.

73. Williamson, *History of the State of Maine*, vol. II, 132.

74. Calvert, *Black Robe on the Kennebec*, 202.

75. Williamson, *History of the State of Maine*, vol. II, 134.

76. *Documentary History of the State of Maine*, vol. XXIII, ed. Maine Historical Society, James Phinney Baxter, 194.

77. Ibid.

78. Williamson, *History of the State of Maine*, vol. II, 148.

# CHAPTER 5

79. The surveyor of the king's woods was responsible for overseeing the preservation of the eastern white pines for the exclusive use of the Royal Navy as masts. Throughout the eighteenth century, the Crown passed

a series of restrictive acts pertaining to the harvesting of white pine by private interests. The surveyor of the king's woods, in addition to managing the procurement of masts and naval stores, was responsible for enforcing the provisions of the White Pine Acts.

80. Greene, *History of Boothbay*, 110.

81. Woodard, Lobster Coast, 124.

82. Eaton, *Annals of the Town of Warren*, 57.

83. McLennan, *Louisbourg from Its Foundation*, 119.

84. Ibid., 120.

85. Acts and Resolves…, vol. III, 155.

86. *Documentary History of the State of Maine*, vol. XXIII, ed. Maine Historical Society, James Phinney Baxter, 291.

87. Ibid.

88. Ibid., 297.

89. Williamson, *History of the State of Maine*, vol. II, 218.

90. *Documentary History of the State of Maine*, vol. XXIII, ed. Maine Historical Society, James Phinney Baxter, 299.

91. Ibid.

92. Rawlyk, *Yankees at Louisburg*, 171. Bradstreet indicates in his own journal that he spoke with Shirley regarding an attack against Louisbourg in December 1744.

93. *Correspondence of William Shirley*, vol. I, 151–52.

94. William Goold in *Collections of the Maine Historical Society*, vol. VII, 295–96.

95. Vaughn owned a large tract of land encompassing the head of Great Salt Bay, Damariscotta Mills and Damariscotta Lake. Damariscotta Mills formed the nucleus of his commercial center, where he erected a double sawmill, a gristmill and his personal residence.

96. *Correspondence of William Shirley*, vol. I, 159–60.

97. Parkman, *Half Century of Conflict*, vol. II, 82.

98. Ibid., 83.

99. Williamson, *History of the State of Maine*, vol. II, 219.

100. By law, all males between the age of sixteen and sixty, with few exceptions, were required to enroll with their local militia company. By the time of King George's War, the militia had become more of an administrative apparatus than an actual military unit to be called into active duty. Serving as a draft board, the province of Massachusetts used the militia companies as a mechanism through which men were selected for provincial service. See Eames, *Rustic Warriors*, 26–29.

101. Acts and Resolves…, vol. XIII, 488.

102. Ibid.
103. Eaton, *History of Thomaston*, 57.
104. Stahl, *History of Old Broad Bay*, 146–49.
105. Williamson, *History of the State of Maine*, vol. II, 247.
106. Ibid.
107. Ibid., 248.
108. Ibid.
109. Johnston, *History of the Towns of Bristol and Bremen*, 294. Johnston's estimation may be misleading. He claims that several people were killed at Walpole and fifteen taken captive. He goes on to state that upriver at Newcastle, several more were killed and thirteen taken captive. While the specific names of those killed are different, leading to the belief that these were separate incidents, it is entirely possible that he was using local oral tradition when writing about the incidents and that they were really one and the same attack.
110. Ibid., 295.
111. Ibid.
112. Eaton, *Annals of the Town of Warren*, 77.
113. Hutchinson, *History of the Province of Massachusetts-Bay*, 435.

# CHAPTER 6

114. Penhallow, *History of the Wars of New England*, 124.
115. Samuel Ball and Benjamin Ledite both served as soldiers during King George's War. Ball's father arrived in the Wiscasset area in 1735 and established a home on the western side of the Sheepscot River near the falls in present Alna. Upon establishing his homestead, Ball's father was threatened and warned out of his holding by the resident native population. Ball's father did not submit to the threats, and in 1747, he was killed and the homestead burned by native warriors.
116. Harnden was investigated for his complicity in Ball's and Ledite's escapes. Several of his assistants accused Harnden of not chasing after the two escapees. Harnden indicated that a snowstorm prevented the pursuit of the fugitives. On January 2, 1749/50, Harnden was cleared of all suspicion in the breakout. Thirteen people were later interviewed as potential suspects. None of those interviewed was subsequently charged.
117. *Documentary History of the State of Maine*, vol. XXIII, ed. Maine Historical Society, James Phinney Baxter, 347.

118. Henry O'Thayer, "A Page of Indian History: The Wiscasset Tragedy," in *Collections of the Maine Historical Society*, Second Series, vol. X, 85.

119. *Documentary History of the State of Maine*, vol. XXIII, ed. Maine Historical Society, James Phinney Baxter, 327.

120. Ibid., 328.

121. Ibid., 329.

122. O'Thayer, "Page of Indian History," 94.

123. *Documentary History of the State of Maine*, vol. XII, ed. Maine Historical Society, James Phinney Baxter, 74.

124. Ibid., 81.

125. Ibid., 92.

126. Ibid., 104–5.

127. Ghere and Morrison, "Searching for Justice," 378–99.

128. Henry O'Thayer, "The Indians Administration of Justice: Sequel to the Wiscasset Tragedy," in *Collections of the Maine Historical Society*, Second Series, vol. X, 193–200.

129. Griffin, "Samuel Ball." Ball did not disappear from the historic record. He resided on the midcoast for the remainder of his life. Ball is recorded as residing on what is now Southport Island before purchasing Squirrel Island off Boothbay Harbor. Ball later played an instrumental role in the establishment of Balltown (Jefferson) following the Revolution.

130. O'Thayer, "Indians Administration of Justice," 100.

131. Ibid.

132. Ibid., 101.

133. Ghere and Morrison, "Searching for Justice," 388–89.

134. Ibid., 391.

# CHAPTER 7

135. *Correspondence of William Shirley*, vol. 2, 12–13.

136. Joseph Williamson, "Materials for a History of Fort Halifax," in *Collections of the Maine Historical Society*, vol. VII, 167.

137. *Documentary History of the State of Maine*, vol. XXIV, Maine Historical Society, ed. Baxter, 9–11. This is the report of Samuel Goodwin. It is but one of several reports regarding the possibility of other French forts being built.

138. Ibid., vol. XII, 248–49.

139. Ibid., 251.

140. Ibid., 252.

141. Anderson, *War That Made America*, 29.

142. Ibid., 31.

143. Williamson, "Materials for a History of Fort Halifax," 218.

144. Ibid.

145. Tortora, *Fort Halifax*, 15.

146. Kershaw, *Kennebec Proprietors*, 134.

147. *Documentary History of the State of Maine*, vol. XII, ed. Maine Historical Society, James Phinney Baxter, 246.

148. Kershaw, *Kennebec Proprietors*, 125.

149. *Documentary History of the State of Maine*, vol. XII, ed. Maine Historical Society, James Phinney Baxter, 362–63.

150. Ibid., 391.

151. William and John Ross, who were taken captive in 1750 following the trial of Obadiah Albee, were seized again along with three other men while prepping fields for planting in the open salvo of the sixth Indian war in 1755.

152. *Documentary History of the State of Maine*, vol. XXIV, ed. Maine Historical Society, James Phinney Baxter, 31.

153. Ibid., 83.

154. *Boston Gazette and Country Journal*, June 23, 1755.

155. *Documentary History of the State of Maine*, vol. XXIV, ed. Maine Historical Society, James Phinney Baxter, 37.

156. Ibid., 35.

157. Ibid.

158. *Boston Gazette and Country Journal*, July 14, 1755.

159. *Documentary History of the State of Maine*, vol. XXIV, ed. Maine Historical Society, James Phinney Baxter, 63; also Spencer Phips's Proclamation Broadside. The same language had been used at least as far back as the declaration of war against the other eastern tribes in June 1755.

160. Captain Cox, operating a schooner out of Falmouth, did take two scalps while cruising the shore of Penobscot Bay. The expenses of outfitting the schooners used to range the coast were covered through individuals who essentially bought stock in the cruises, paying for the upfront costs in anticipation of receiving their portion of any scalp bounties claimed.

161. *Documentary History of the State of Maine*, vol. XXIV, ed. Maine Historical Society, James Phinney Baxter, 72. Bradbury enquired of twenty-one native leaders by name. Of those, fourteen had succumbed to the ravages of smallpox.

162. Ibid. It is interesting to note that the phrase "we the old men of Penobscutt" is used in the letter. This seems to reflect continued intergenerational divides between the Penobscot people.

163. Ibid., 73.

164. Ibid., 82.

165. Ibid., vol. XIII, 102.

166. Ibid., 128–31.

167. Boishebert saw more than a decade of service as an officer in the Troupes d' la Marine during King George's War and Father Loutre's war as part of the Acadian resistance to British rule in Nova Scotia. Boishebert had recently participated in the defense of Louisbourg and would go on to serve in the defense of Quebec.

168. On May 23, 1759, Waldo dropped dead while scouting the Penobscot River near present Brewer. Waldo stood to benefit immensely from the expansion of the Maine frontier and his own Waldo Patent.

169. "Governor Pownall's Journal of His Voyage from Boston to Penobscot River, May 1759," in *Collections of the Maine Historical Society*, vol. V, 376.

170. *Documentary History of the State of Maine*, vol. XXIV, ed. Maine Historical Society, James Phinney Baxter, 159.

# Bibliography

## PUBLISHED WORKS

*The Acts and Resolves, Public and Private, of the Province of Massachusetts Bay*. Vol. I. Boston: Wright and Potter Printing Co., 1869.

———. Vol. III. Boston: Wright and Potter Printing Co., 1878.

———. Vol. VII. Boston: Wright and Potter Printing Co., 1892.

———. Vol. VIII. Boston: Wright and Potter Printing Co., 1895.

———. Vol. IX. Boston: Wright and Potter Printing Co., 1902.

———. Vol. XII. Boston: Wright and Potter Printing Co., 1905.

———. Vol. XIV. Boston: Wright and Potter Printing Co., 1907.

———. Vol. XV. Boston: Wright and Potter Printing Co., 1908.

———. Vol. XVI. Boston: Wright and Potter Printing Co., 1909.

Allen, Charles E. *The History of Dresden, Maine*. Augusta, ME: Kennebec Journal Print Shop, 1931.

Anderson, Fred. *Crucible of War: The Seven Years War and the Fate of Empire in British North America, 1754–1766*. New York: Vintage Books, 2000.

———. *The War That Made America*. New York, 2005.

Baker, Emerson W., et al, eds. *American Beginnings: Exploration, Culture, and Cartography in the Land of Norumbega*. Lincoln: University of Nebraska Press, 1994.

Baker, William Avery. *A Maritime History of Bath, Maine and the Kennebec River Region*. Portland, ME: Anthoensen Press, 1973.

Bourne, Edward E., LLD. *The History of Wells and Kennebunk*. Portland, ME: Thurston & Company, n.d.

Bourque, Bruce. *Twelve Thousand Years: American Indians in Maine*. Lincoln: University of Nebraska Press, 2001.

Brack, H.G. *Norumbega Reconsidered: Mawooshen and the Wawenoc Diaspora*. Liberty, ME: Pennywheel Press, 2008.

Bradley, Robert L., and Helen B. Camp. *The Forts of Pemaquid, Maine: An Archaeological and Historical Study*. Augusta: Maine Historic Preservation Commission, 1994.

Burrage, Henry S. *Maine at Louisburg in 1745*. Augusta, ME: Burleigh & Flynt, 1910.

Calvert, Mary R. *Black Robe on the Kennebec*. Monmouth, ME: Monmouth Press, 1991.

Chase, Fannie S. *Wiscasset in Pownalborough: A History of the Shire Town and the Salient Historical Features of the Territory Between the Sheepscot and Kennebec Rivers*. Wiscasset, ME, 1941.

*The Correspondence of William Shirley*. New York: Macmillan Co., 1912.

Cronon, William. *Changes in the Land: Indians, Colonists, and the Ecology of New England*. New York: Hill and Wang, 1983.

Cushman, Reverend David Quimby. *The History of Ancient Sheepscot and Newcastle*. Bath, ME: E. Upton and Sons, 1882.

Drake, James D. *King Philip's War: Civil War in New England, 1675–1676*. Amherst: University of Massachusetts Press, 1999.

Drake, Samuel Adams. *The Border Wars of New England: Commonly Called King William's and Queen Anne's Wars*. New York: Charles Scribner's Sons, 1897.

Eames, Steven C. *Rustic Warriors: Warfare and the Provincial Soldier on the New England Frontier, 1689–1748*. New York: New York University Press, 2011.

Eaton, Cyrus. *Annals of the Town of Warren*. Hallowell, ME: Masters and Livermore, 1877.

———. *History of Thomaston, Rockland and South Thomaston, Maine*. Hallowell, ME: Masters, Smith & Co., 1865.

Fischer, Davis Hacket: *Albion's Seed: Four British Folkways in America*. New York: Oxford University Press, 1989.

Fowler, William, Jr. *Empires at War: The French and Indian War and the Struggle for North America, 1754–1763*. New York: Walker and Company, 2005.

Ghere, David L., and Alvin Morrison. "Searching for Justice on the Maine Frontier: Legal Concepts, Treaties and the 1749 Wiscasset Incident." *American Indian Quarterly* 25, no. 3 (Summer 2001): 378–99.

Goold, William. *Portland in the Past with Historical Notes of Old Falmouth*. Portland, ME: Thurston & Company, 1886.

Greene, Byron Francis. *History of Boothbay, Southport and Boothbay Harbor, Maine*. Portland, ME: Loring Short and Harmon, 1906.

Gyles, John. *Memoirs of Odd Adventures, Strange Deliverances, &c. in the Captivity of John Gyles Esq; Commander of the Garrison on Saint George River*. Boston: S. Kneeland and T. Green, 1736.

Haefeli, Evan, and Kevin Sweeny. *Captive Histories: English, French and Native Narratives of the 1704 Deerfield Raid*. Amherst: University of Massachusetts Press, 2006.

————. *Captors and Captives: The 1704 French and Indian Raid on Deerfield*. Amherst: University of Massachusetts Press, 2003.

Hutchinson, Thomas. *The History of the Province of Massachusetts-Bay*. Boston: Thomas & John Fleet, 1767.

Johnston, A.B.J. *The Summer of 1744: A Portrait of Life in 18ᵗʰ Century Louisbourg*. Hull, Quebec: Parks Canada, 1983.

Johnston, John, LLD. *A History of the Towns of Bristol and Bremen, in the State of Maine*. Albany, NY: Joel Munsell, 1873.

Judd, Richard William, Edwin A. Churchill and Joel W. Eastman. *Maine: The Pine Tree State from Prehistory to the Present*. Orono: University of Maine, 1995.

Kershaw, Gordon. *Kennebec Proprietors*. Portland: Maine Historical Society, 1975.

Leamon, James S. *Revolution Downeast: The War for American Independence in Maine*. Amherst: University of Massachusetts Press, 1993.

Leyburn, James. *The Scotch Irish: A Social History*. Chapel Hill: University of North Carolina Press, 1989.

Maine Historical Society. *Collections of the Maine Historical Society*. Second Series, vol. V. Portland, ME: Brown Thurston, 1894.

————. *Collections of the Maine Historical Society*. Second Series, vol. X. Portland, ME: Thurston Print, 1899.

————. *Collections of the Maine Historical Society*. Vol. V. Portland, ME: Brown Thurston, 1855.

————. *Collections of the Maine Historical Society*. Vol. VI. Portland, ME: Brown Thurston, 1859.

————. Collections of the Maine Historical Society. Vol. VII. Bath, ME: E. Upton and Son, 1876.

————. Collections of the Maine Historical Society. Vol. VIII. Portland, ME: Hoyt, Fogg & Dunham, 1881.

————. *Documentary History of the State of Maine.* Vol. IX. Portland, ME: LeFavor-Tower Co., 1907.

————. *Documentary History of the State of Maine.* Vol. X. Portland, ME: LeFavor-Tower Co., 1907.

————. *Documentary History of the State of Maine.* Vol. XI. Portland, ME: LeFavor-Tower Co., 1908.

————. *Documentary History of the State of Maine.* Vol. XII. Portland, ME: LeFavor-Tower Co., 1908.

————. *Documentary History of the State of Maine.* Vol. XIII. Portland, ME: LeFavor-Tower Co., 1908.

————. *Documentary History of the State of Maine.* Vol. XXIII. Portland, ME: Fred L. Tower Co., 1916.

————. *Documentary History of the State of Maine.* Vol. XXIV. Portland, ME: Fred L. Tower Co., 1916.

McLennan, J.S. *Louisbourg from Its Foundation to Its Fall, 1713–1758.* London: MacMillan and Co., 1918.

Owen, Henry Wilson, AB. *History of Bath, Maine.* Bath, ME: Times Company, 1916.

Parker, Arlita Dodge. *A History of Pemaquid.* Boston: MacDonald and Evan, 1925.

Parkman, Count Francis. *Frontenac and New France Under Louis XIV.* France and England in North America, Part V. Boston: Little, Brown and Company, 1910.

————. *A Half Century of Conflict.* France and England in North America, Part VI, vol. I. Boston: Little Brown and Company, 1902.

————. *A Half Century of Conflict.* France and England in North America, Part VI, vol. II. Boston: Little Brown and Company, 1924.

Penhallow, Samuel. *The History of the Wars of New England, with the Eastern Indians.* Boston: T. Fleet, 1726.

Plummer, Edward Clarence. *History of Bath, Maine.* New York: Times Company, 1936.

Rawlyk, G.A. *Yankees at Louisbourg.* Orono: University of Maine Press, 1967.

Reed, Barbara Freeman. *Colonial Muster Rolls of Maine Forts and Towns, 1700–1760.* Boothbay Harbor, ME, 1964.

Rumsey, Barbara. *Colonial Boothbay, Mid 1600's to 1775.* East Boothbay, ME: Winnegance House, 2000.

Shultz, Eric B., and Michael Tougias. *King Philip's War: The History and Legacy of America's Forgotten Conflict.* Woodstock, VT: Countryman Press, 1999.

Stahl, Jasper J. *History of Old Broad Bay and Waldoboro.* Vol. I. Portland, ME: Bond Wheelright Company, 1956.

Tortora, Daniel. *Fort Halifax: Winslow's Historic Outpost.* Charleston, SC: The History Press, 2014.

Webb, James. *Born Fighting: How the Scots Irish Shaped America.* New York: Broadway Books, 2004.

Wheeler, George Augustus, and Henry Warren Wheeler. *The History of Brunswick, Topsham and Harpswell, Maine.* Boston: Alfred Mudge & Sons Printer, 1878.

Williamson, William D. *The History of the State of Maine.* Hallowell, ME: Glazer, Masters & Co., 1832.

Woodard, Collin. *The Lobster Coast: Rebels, Rusticators and the Struggle for a Forgotten Frontier*. New York: Viking, 1989.


# UNPUBLISHED MANUSCRIPTS

Baker, Emerson W. "Trouble to the Eastward: The Failure of Anglo-Indian Relations in Early Maine." PhD dissertation, College of William and Mary, 1986.

Griffin, Chip. "Samuel Ball 1729–1800: Mid Coast Hell Raiser and Squirrel Island Settler." Presentation to the Squirrel Islanders, Boothbay Harbor, ME. August 4, 2011.

Lozier, Jean Francois. "In Each Other's Arms: France and the Saint Lawrence Mission Villages in War and Peace, 1630–1730." PhD dissertation, University of Toronto, 2012.

Massachusetts Archives volumes of original documents.


# NEWSPAPERS

*Boston Evening Post*, September 4, 1758.

*Boston Gazette and Country Journal*, June 23, 1755; July 14, 1755; August 28, 1758.

*Boston News Letter*, August 31, 1758.

*Boston Post Boy*, September 4, 1758.

# *Index*

# About the Author

Growing up and residing in midcoast Maine, Mike Dekker has developed a lifelong passion for the region's past. An avid student of eighteenth-century American history and material culture, he presents educational programs for local historical societies, state historic sites, schools and the public. Portraying Maine soldiers of the French and Indian War and the American Revolution as a living historian, Mike endeavors to relate the stories of forgotten individuals and their world.

*Visit us at*
www.historypress.net
........................................................
*This title is also available as an e-book*